HUMAN RIGHTS AND LAW ENFORCEMENT

About the Author

Sankar Sen, former Director General, National Human Rights Commission, New Delhi and former Director of the National Police Academy, Hyderabad, joined the Indian Police Service in 1960. He graduated from Presidency College, Calcutta and obtained Master's degree in History from the Calcutta University. He was allotted to Orissa cadre and held a number of posts with distinction. He joined the Border Security Force as the Inspector General in 1987 and was later on promoted as the Additional Director General. Thereafter, he was posted as the Director of the SVP National Police Academy (NPA), the premier institution for training of the senior police officers in the country. As the Director of the NPA, he was responsible for many innovative changes in the training curricula of the police officers.

He was awarded the Police Medal for Meritorious Service in 1979 and President's Police Medal for Distinguished Service in 1986. On completion of his assignment in the NPA, he joined as the Director General of the National Human Rights Commission and later on functioned as the Special Rapporteur, in charge of custodial programmes of the NHRC. His books— *Police Today* and *Human Rights in a Developing Society* won great acclaim from the law enforcement officers, human rights activists and informed members of the public.

HUMAN RIGHTS
AND
LAW ENFORCEMENT

Sankar Sen, *IPS*

CONCEPT PUBLISHING COMPANY, NEW DELHI-110059

ISBN : 81-7022-979-0

First Published 2002

Published and Printed by
Ashok Kumar Mittal
Concept Publishing Company
A/15-16, Commercial Block, Mohan Garden,
New Delhi-110059

Phones : 5351460, 5351794
Fax : 091-11-5357103
E-mail : publishing@conceptpub.com

PREF/ ...

The book, containing twelve articles, deals with some important issues of law enforcement and human rights concern in the country. These articles appeared in national dailies and in journals in and outside the country Thoughts and views expressed in these articles had been the outcome of my experience gathered and insights gained during long years spent in the sphere of law enforcement and my stint as the Director General of the National Human Rights Commission. Problems of policing a democratic society are complex and varied, but I am of the firm view that the hallmark of good policing is and should be concern for and protection of human rights while waging a relentless battle against crime and disorder. Order is to be maintained through law—not always an easy job. In the present endeavour on human rights issues, I have tried to highlight the need for tackling these deep-seated societal issues with a sense of urgency and commitment.

I hope that this bunch of articles will evoke interest among thc acadcmics, law cnforccmcnt officcrs and human rights groups and will be of some help in evolving strategies to effectively deal with them. I am grateful to Mr. C.R. Ram Editor, *Statesman*, for giving permission vide his letter dated.....to use some of my articles earlier published in the *Statesman*.

Sankar Sen

1st Proof

CONTENTS

SECTION I

1

LAW ENFORCEMENT AND CIVIL SERVICES*

The preamble of the Indian Constitution declares the solemn resolve of the Indian people to constitute India into a sovereign socialist secular democratic republic and to secure to all its citizens "social, economic and political justice and equality of status and opportunity and fraternity assuring the dignity of the individual and the unity and integrity of the nation". To give effect to the ideals enshrined in the preamble, the Constitution incorporates Fundamental Rights in Part-III and Directive Principles in Part-IV of the Constitution. Article 13(2) of the Constitution declares that "the State shall not make any law which takes away or abridges the Fundamental Rights. Any law made in contravention of this clause shall be void". The fundamental rights had been described by Dr. Radhakrishnan, former President of India, as "a pledge to our people and a pact with the civilised world". The fundamental rights are the natural rights to life, liberty, security of person, protection against discriminatory and arbitrary arrest which find place in the Universal Declaration of Human Rights as quintessential human rights.

In this connection, it can be mentioned that the Universal Declaration of Human Rights was adopted by the United Nations General Assembly when debates in the Indian Constituent Assembly for the drafting of the Constitution were going on. Hence, it must be assumed, as the Supreme Court has said in the case of Menaka Gandhi Vs Union of India, that the makers of the Indian Constitution in framing Part-III on the Fundamental

---

* Appeared in The Statesman on 24-12-2000.

Rights were influenced by the provisions of the Universal Declaration. The Supreme Court has in an expansive interpretation further stated that "not only Fundamental Rights but also Directive Principles are based on human rights so that "the directives, even though non-justiciable, are not to be regarded as inferior to the Fundamental Rights".[1]

However, protection and promotion of fundamental rights depend on proper and efficient law enforcement. Only through proper enforcement of rules and laws orderly civilised society can function and the majesty of its institutions can be upheld. The quality and manner of law enforcement is often indicative of the quality of governance. It is aptly said that the difference between the democracy and a dictatorship is not in the laws but in the manner of enforcement of the laws. In a democratic system laws have to be enforced not only firmly but also with due regard to the rights of the citizens. In the name of efficient law enforcement fundamental rights of the citizens cannot be chilled.

Effective law enforcement is possible only when there are trained and efficient keepers of the law wedded to human rights norms. Article 312 of the Constitution created two All-India Services—Indian Administrative and the Indian Police Services and contained provisions for creation of more All-India Services "if necessary or expedient in the national interest to do so". Sardar Patel, India's first Home Minister, who has often been described as India's Bismarck, had the vision to see from the beginning that no democratic government will be effective without "well-organised, well-paid and independent civil service". It was a year ahead of independence that Sardar Patel got a resolution adopted by the Congress Chief Ministers authorising Constitution of two All-India Services (IAS and IPS). He could foresee that these two services would contribute to the unity of the country and strengthen the administrative structure with high standards of probity and uniformity. He also felt that the civil services should be given as much independence as possible and carried his point against great opposition in the Constituent Assembly. "For the first time since the Maurayan bureaucracy there was

1. Minerva Mills *Vs* Union of India - 1980 S.C. 1989 (paras 11- 12).

established the uniform administration from which no part of the country was excluded and never before had the country been unified as an unrestricted democracy in which all citizens had equal political and other rights"[2] Sardar Patel said in the Constituent Assembly in October 1949, that "we will not have a united India if we do not have good All-India Service which had independence to speak its own mind. If you do not adopt the course then do not follow the present Constitution, substitute it for something else".

With the passage of time serious problems in law enforcement began to surface, which were not visualised by the Founding Fathers of the Constitution. In a democracy, it is the responsibility of the civil service, the magistracy, the police and judiciary to enforce laws in an impartial and non-partisan manner. It is here now difficulties are being encountered. Immediately after independence the quality and calibre of political leaders were high and they were animated by a sense of idealism. But very soon the new breed of political leaders came on the scene who were not interested in impartial implementation of the laws. They want that laws should be implemented in a manner that will help their friends, relations and political supporters. This causes acute problems for honest and independent law enforcement officers. So, politicians now prefer officers who are not upright and strong-willed and are willing to function as "sycophants and courtiers" (to quote the well-known phrases of the renowned civil servant Dharam Vira).

Extraneous Interference

In dealing with undue extraneous interference in law enforcement particularly in the exercise of the discretionary authority and statutory duties of the police, the National Police Commission quoted the following observation of Prof. David Bayley.[3]

"In India today a dual system of criminal justice has grown

2. Problem of Policing in India, L.P. Singh, Sardar Patel Memorial Lectures—NPA Publication. p. 86
3. *Police and Political Development in India.* David Bayley

> up—the one of law, the other of politics. With respect, at least, to the police, decisions made by the police officials about the application of law are frequently subject to partisan review or direction by elected representatives. This autonomy of police officials in specific and routine applications of law has been severely curtailed. This is not only true of law and order situations. People accused of crimes have grown into the habit of appealing to political figures for remission from the sanctions of law. Police officers throughout India have grown accustomed to calculating the likely political effect of any enforcement action they contemplate. Fearing for their careers, and especially their postings, they have become anxious and cynical... But everywhere officers expect to be held personally accountable by politicians even more than by superior officers for enforcement actions taken in the course of duty."

He has further observed

> "Altogether, then, the rule of law in modern India, the frame upon which justice hangs, has been undermined by the rule of politics. Supervision in the name of democracy has eroded the foundations upon which impartiality depends in a criminal justice system".

Kerala Police Commission, 1959 also referred to the malady of political interference and observed that "the greatest obstacles to efficient police administration flows from the domination of party politics under the State administration. The result of partisan interference is often reflected in lawless enforcement of laws, inferior service and in general decline of police prestige followed by irresponsible criticism and consequential widening of the cleavage between the police and the public, affecting the confidence of the public in the integrity and objectives of the police force."

The Federal system, established by the Constitution, presents another set of problems for law enforcement. Under the

Constitution, public order and police are State subjects and yet failure of the police to deal with the law and order problems or commission of excesses are often raised in the Parliament. Attempts to bar discussions on ground of constitutional limitation do not always succeed. There are also many occasions when the judgement of the Central government about handling of a major political law and order problem is totally different from that of the State government. Consequently, the civil servants find difficult to satisfy two masters and fall between the two stools.

Escalation of Crime and Lawlessness

Again, with the passage of years there is escalation of crime and lawlessness. One of the basic objectives of effective law enforcement is to maintain peace and tranquillity in the country so that people can pursue their vocations without being haunted by the fear of crime and lawlessness. It is aptly said that after war, crime is the biggest disintegrating force in modern societies. In India, with the passing of every decade, there is steady increase of crime and lawlessness. In the year 1997, 64.11 lakh cognisable crimes were reported. This marks 28.3 per cent increase over the figures of 1987. Twelve cognisable crimes are now reported on an average every minute. The rate of crime, defined as the incidence of crime per one lakh of population, is universally taken as a realistic indicator. The rate of crime in 1996 was 675.6, an increase of 17.9 per cent over 1986. Statistics, however, do not reveal the correct picture of the situation. According to criminologists and knowledgeable law enforcement officers, the reported crime in Indian context is almost one-tenth of the actual incidence. Even these concealed crime figures also show a sharp escalation of crimes against women and other forms of violent crimes. During the last three years, there had been a steadily increasing trend in violent crimes against life (from 95,939 in 1995 to 98,638 in 1997) and violent crimes directed towards women (from 13,754 in 1995 to 15,330 in 1997).

Non-Registration of Cases

It is also a fact that massive burking of crime takes place. Large number of cases in police stations are not registered. This, apart from being a serious violation of human rights, has a very negative impact on law enforcement. Discussing this evil practice of non-registration of complaints at police stations, the National Police Commission in its Fourth Report (Page 1 and 2) said the following :

> "This malpractice of non-registration arises from several factors, including the extraneous influences and corruption that operate on the system, besides the disinclination of the staff to take on additional load of investigational work in the midst of heavy pressure of several other duties. Among all such factors the most important one, which, in our view, accounts for a substantial volume of crime going unregistered, is the anxiety of the political executive in the State Government to keep the recorded crime figures low so as to claim before the State Legislature, the public and the press that crime is well controlled and is even going down as a result of 'efficient' police administration under their charge. The Chiefs of Police and other senior police officers also find it easy and convenient to toe the line of the Government in developing such a statistical approach for assessing the crime situation and evaluating police performance. As a consequence, this attitude permeates the entire hierarchy down the line and is reflected at the police stations in their reluctance and refusal to register cases as and when crimes are brought to their notice."

In this connection it may be mentioned that the second West Bengal Police Commission undertook a field survey of police-society relationship and came across some revealing truths. It found that starting from the stage of lodging a complaint in the police station one had to take the help of the political person without which no complaint would be registered. In a survey conducted by it, as much as 77 per cent of the respondents had to take the help of either member of an "elected body" or "non-elected influential person" to get their complaints registered. The survey report states "when we ask our respondents under which type of circumstances does it become difficult to take action against the criminals, once again the finger is pointed towards the politicians. Policemen find it most difficult to take action against criminals when they are politically connected".

Delay in Disposal of Cases

Another major reason for the sharp escalation of crime is that criminals have come to realise that the crime pays and the gains of crime outweigh the risks of crime. After all, it is not the severity but the certainty of the punishment that deters the criminals. The criminal justice system in order to be effective must function with speed. Unfortunately, in various courts of the country there is a staggering number of cases pending at various stages of adjudication. The right to speedy trial has been recognised by the Supreme Court as a part of the protection available under Article 21 of the Constitution. But the pronouncements of the Supreme Court, unfortunately, have remained on paper. According to official statistics, out of 5.3 million IPC cases pending in the year 1996, only 0.8 million were finalised. In other words, the courts take almost 6.6 years to finalise a case. Because of this long delay, the witnesses become tired and fed up with irksome processes of the trial court. Many of them die or are bought over. No wonder that under these circumstances 75 per cent of the accused persons are acquitted. In heinous offences and in corruption cases the rate of conviction is less than 10 per cent. "As many as 70 per cent of the involved litigants are from the villages. The longer a case runs the more expensive it is to pursue it."[4] The Mumbai bomb blast case of 1993 is not likely to be decided before 2005 in the trial court. Thereafter appeals will take perhaps another 20 to 30 years. Recently in a speech on the occasion of the Golden Jubilee Celebrations of the Supreme Court, K.R.Narayanan, President of India, emphasised the need for accountable judiciary in India dispensing quick, affordable and incorruptible justice to the people. He felt that "without access to unpolluted, expeditious

4. Human Development in South Asia, 1999. The Crisis of Governance, page 66

and inexpensive justice the people, instead of taking recourse to law, may be tempted to take law in their own hands." It is also a fact that sharp increase in the number of cases in the courts have not been matched by an increase in the number of judges. "There are only 10 to 12 judges for every million people in the country, while advanced countries had almost 50 judges per million. In those countries hardly 7 to 10 per cent of litigation goes for trial, the rest are settled out of court" However, paucity of judges is not the only problem. "Judicial administration", as one distinguished Professor of Law put it "is yet untouched by the management revolution of the 20th century and information revolution of the present century. There is not much evidence to show that somebody in the profession or in the judiciary is disturbed by the situation."[5]

Over-Proliferation of Laws

Another related aspect that impinges on effective law enforcement is over-proliferation of laws. A vast number of old and outdated laws clutter the statute books. A Commission appointed by the Central Government concluded that over 1200 central laws were out of date and either needed to be repealed altogether or suitably amended. It is a crowning pity that most of the State governments have not even undertaken the exercise to identify laws which have no utility. Time and again, it has been noticed that punishments prescribed by the laws are so nominal as not to have any effect on the crime situation. It is a waste of time to carry out elaborate time-consuming court proceedings resulting in a fine of few rupees or simple imprisonment for a few days. Such penal provisions have to be amended to provide deterrent punishment for the offenders. The Law Commission recommended American system of plea-bargaining in India for speedy conclusion of the criminal cases. It is time that the court procedures are simplified and laws rewritten to serve the interests of the litigants and not the lawyers.

---

5. Article on "Criminal Justice" by Dr. Madhava Menon in *The Statesman* dated 14.09.2000

It can be seen that scores of reports of the Law Commission for amendment of laws are lying unattended for years. And even when the government approves a bill for amending any act, Parliament/ State Legislature has no time to attend to legislative business. In this connection specific mention may be made of the provision for grant of anticipatory bail in the Criminal Procedure Code. Such provision does not exist in UK, USA and in some other countries. This provision has often been misused; people with money and power have made use of this provision to avoid arrest and interrogation in police custody. Several decisions of the courts granting bail to the accused have raised eyebrows. It is time that this provision is altogether abolished.

Police Reforms

Again, law enforcement by the police cannot improve without basic structural reforms in the police to insulate it from external pressures and influence. The Police Act of 1861 created a ruler appointed police which served as the defender of the establishment with servility towards the ruler and alienation from the public. The same Police Act rules the roost even now and political masters have shown no anxiety to bring about structural reforms in the police. The salient recommendations of the National Police Commission, which were also strongly endorsed by the National Human Rights Commission, have remained unimplemented. Indrajit Gupta, the then Union Home Minister, in a letter to the Chief Ministers said the following:

> It is sad a commentary on our professed commitment to the people to provide them with a professionally competent and reasonably clean police administration that we have so far not even made any serious attempt to implement many of the basic and salutary re-commendations of the National Police Commission to bring about the required changes in police performance and behaviour pattern. On the contrary, quite often the recommendations of the NPC for police reforms have been misrepresented, perhaps deliberately, as amounting

> to giving unbridled power to the police. In reality, however, proper implementation of the recommendations will amount to not only curbing many of the existing powers of misuse by the police but also by those who are the existing controllers of the police, viz., the political executives and the bureaucracy. The proposed reforms will reduce to the minimum the possible misuse of powers, both by the policemen of themselves and also by their controllers by introducing more effective systems of checks and balances and also by ensuring discharge of police functions strictly in accordance with law and professional requirements without fear or favour. It will also ensure greater transparency, accountability and responsiveness to public criticism of police functioning.

He also said that "I have a feeling if political executives do not take desired measures even now to bring about suggested reforms and restructuring of the police, the day may not be far off when the judiciary may intervene decisively to force such socially desirable changes down the throat of political executives."

A case is now pending before the Supreme Court (Prakash Singh *Vs* Union of India, Writ Petition No. 310 of 1996) for issuing speedy directions for the implementation of the recommendations of the National Police Commission. The National Human Rights Commission has also impleaded itself in the case and given its submission for implementation of the important recommendations of the Commission. It has been pointed out by the NHRC that systemic reforms in police are essential for protection and promotion of human rights.

Politician-Civil Service-Police Nexus

Meanwhile, another horrendous development has taken place. There has been steady growth of a nexus between bureaucrats, politicians and criminals — *babu, neta, dada* syndrome. The country is today witnessing a disturbing spectacle of politicisation of crime and criminalisation of politics. The report of the Vora

Committee recognises this ominous trend of criminal, political and bureaucratic nexus assuming alarming proportions. The report warns the people of "sinister linkages between underworld, politicians and bureaucracy. Some political leaders become the leaders of these gangs and over the years get themselves elected to the local bodies, State assemblies and Parliament. Resultantly, such elements have acquired considerable political clout, as a result jeopardising the smooth functioning of the administration and the safety of life and the property of the common man, causing a sense of despair and alienation among the people." This noxious development, combined with the politicisation of the police, poses real threats to the survival of the democratic society. It also nullifies law enforcement and makes law enforcement apparatus irrelevant. Many powerful criminals today, instead of playing the role of king-makers behind the scene, are jumping in the arena of politics and becoming political leaders themselves. To counter this ominous trend some electoral reforms are called for. It is necessary that persons involved in grave criminal offences, as identified and notified by the Election Commission, should be banned from fighting elections if charges have been framed against them. This responsibility can be cast on the candidate and he must be asked to certify that he has not been charged for any criminal offence in law courts and provide details.

Distrust of the Police

Our criminal laws brand the police as untrustworthy. Section 25 of the Indian Evidence Act makes confessions before a police officer inadmissible in evidence as also Section 161 of the Criminal Procedure Code makes statement before the police officers inadmissible. Thus, though the police remain responsible for controlling crime and securing conviction of the criminals, they are deprived of the right to secure and use confessions, even when they are voluntarily made, as they are in a large number of cases. So they go to circumvent laws and resort to various measures, often irregular and illegal, to secure conviction.

The Law Commission of India in its 14th Report recommended that Section 25 of the Evidence Act might be amended and police officers of and above the rank of DSP should be empowered to record the confessions of the accused. It is amazing that even 128 years after the Act was passed, evidence before the superior, well-educated police officers are considered as inadmissible in evidence, though statements given to Excise officers and officers of the Enforcement Directorate can be used as evidence under the Indian Evidence Act. It is a curious anomaly that while law gives wide powers to a police officer to arrest anyone and keep him under custody for at least 24 hours, it goes to place unreasonable restrictions on the testimony of the police officers. Sections 161, 162 and 164 of the CrPC and Sections 25, 26 and 27 of the Indian Evidence Act should be recast to remove shackles on the police testimony. No one wants that confession should be relied upon even they are unfairly obtained. All that is wanted is that evidence obtained in such confessions must not be lost to the court which is expected to act on evidence that can withstand the glare of vigorous scrutiny. Section 162 of CrPC provides that those who give statements before the police are not to sign it. This frequently enables witnesses to resile from the statements in the court of law. In England, statement before the police are generally signed and considerable importance is attached to them because it is difficult to confute such statements. Of course, judges should have the discretionary power to exclude evidence which have been unfairly obtained.

Oversight Mechanism

For efficient law enforcement the police have also to be made accountable. Numerous complaints of misuse of force and power by the police are being received by the NHRC and it has been found that many of the complaints have substance in them. The NHRC has also suggested that police autonomy should be matched by police accountability. There should be oversight mechanisms to look into complaints of misuse of authority by the police and speedy action could be taken against the defaulting officers. The NHRC has suggested that there should be mandatory judicial enquiry into all cases of custodial death and rape, setting up District Complaints Authority to examine grievances of the public in matters of misuse of power and custodial violence by the police and introduction of Lay Visitors Scheme for visiting police lock-ups similar to the one introduced in UK in the early 1980s on the recommendations of the Scarman Report. Some civilian review of police conduct in whatever form is essential. Ultimately, the police are responsible to the public and not to the Chief of the Police.

Corruption

Corruption in the civil service is another factor of great concern having a very negative impact on good governance. India today, unfortunately, has become one of the world's most corrupt countries. The Sixth Annual International Perception Index, prepared by the Transparency International, an international NGO based in Berlin, has placed India 69th among the 90 countries, so far corruption is concerned. Corruption is one of the most damaging consequences of poor governance. It also subverts law enforcement and undermines the legitimacy of the state. Entrenched corruption undermines the political and social fabric of a country. Some of the economic theorists have propounded the idea of "multiple equilibria" to explain the incidence of entrenched corruption. Initial conditions are vital. If an economy is jolted to an average level of corruption, it will move towards "the high-corruption equilibrium".

It is a fact that in India the civil servants enjoy various categories of fair procedures which are not available to the counterparts in other countries. Santanam Committee (Report on the Prevention of Corruption, page 34) wrote that in the USA "where it is proposed to dismiss, remove or demote a federal employee, he cannot claim any special trial or hearing. It is granted at the discretion of the department concerned. Such an employee is required to submit a written reply in his defence within five working days. In the U.K. also the disciplinary proceedings are conducted with undue formality, though care is taken that no government servant is punished unless he has been given an opportunity to defend himself In India, while interpreting reasonable opportunity in Article 311 of the Constitution, the courts have laid down that disciplinary proceedings should be conducted in accordance with the tenets of natural justice. The courts have also laid down a number of restrictive conditions. As a result, very few corrupt officials get punished and the public services are being saddled with the men of doubtful integrity. There is considerable weight in the view of the Santanam Committee that "it would not be unreasonable justification to treat departmental proceedings involving charges of bribery, corruption and lack of integrity to a separate category and provide for a simplified procedure."

In this connection, it may be further mentioned that for weeding out corruption in civil service the National Police Commission has suggested that action against the corrupt officers should be taken by availing of the provisions of Article 311(2)(C) of the Constitution. To avoid any doubts regarding the legal propriety of action, it recommended that clause 'C' in the article should be amended to read as "where the President or the Governor, as the case may be, is satisfied that in the interest of the security of the state or maintaining of integrity in the public service it is not expedient to hold such an enquiry."

Despite seemingly entrenched nature of corruption, even now it is not too late to deal effectively with the menace of corruption and shift out of the "high-corruption trap". Many countries, including France in the 19th century to Singapore in the 20th century, have completed the transition from high to low corruption societies. Strong political commitment and a determined anti-corruption agenda and strategy can bring about such a transition in India.

Fifty years have rolled by since the framing of the Constitution. On the eve of country's Independence, Nehru said of the "great triumph and achievements that await us". However, these triumphs and achievements will continue to wait unless the quality of law enforcement improves and the civil servants seek to resolutely work for :

A land of settled government
A land of just and old renown
Where freedom slowly broadens down
From precedent to precedent

—**Tennyson**

2

PENDENCY OF CASES IN THE TRIAL COURTS*

Today, in various courts of the country a staggering number of cases are pending at various stages of adjudication. Recently, Arun Jaitley, Union Law Minister, at a function organised by the Supreme Court Bar Association said that there are 4.04 crore cases pending in District Courts across the country, while there are arrears of 34 lakh cases in High Courts. As many as 70 per cent of these cases involve litigation from the villagers. The longer a case runs the more expensive it becomes to pursue. The President of India, K.R. Narayanan, was absolutely right when he said that "without access to unpolluted, expeditious and inexpensive justice the people, instead of taking recourse to law, may be tempted to take law in their own hands".** The right to speedy trial has been recognised by the Supreme Court as a part of the protection available under Article 21 of the Constitution. The Constitution bench of the Supreme Court in M.S. Sheriff *Vs*. State of Madras held that the public interest demanded that "criminal justice should be swift and sure and the guilty should be punished while the events are fresh in the public mind and that the innocent should be absolved as is consistent with the fair trial. Another reason is that it is undesirable to let things slide till memories have grown too dim to trust". The pronouncements of the Apex Court, however, have not improved the situation on the ground.

The Arrears Committee, headed by Justice V.S. Mallimath

---

* Appeared in *The Statesman* on 4-1-2001 & 5-1-2001.

** Speech of the President of India, K.R. Narayanan, in the Golden Jubilee Celebration of the Supreme Court.

(1990), identified the various causes of accumulation of arrears in the High Courts. Some of the principal causes are, (1) litigation explosion, (2) accumulation of first appeals, (3) inadequacy of the staff attached to the High Courts, (4) inordinate concentration of work in the hands of some members of the Bar, (5) lack of punctuality among the judges, (6) granting of unnecessary adjournments, (7) indiscriminate closure of the courts, (8) indiscriminate resort to writ jurisdiction, (9) inadequacy of classification and granting of cases, and (10) inordinate delay in the supply of certified copies of judgements and orders etc.

It is a fact that increase in the number of cases in the courts have not been matched by an increase in the number of judges. In this respect, the position in India is very much akin to that of other countries of South Asia. This will be clear from the table given below:

Country	No. of persons per judge	No. of cases pending per judge
Bangladesh	94,937	5,142
India	90,909	2,137
Nepal	85,377	314
Pakistan	85,038	454
Sri Lanka	76,339	-
South Asia	90,324	2,170

Source : Human Development in South Asia 1999— The Crisis of Governance.

There are only 10-12 judges for every million people in the country, while advanced countries have 50 judges per million. In those countries hardly 7-10 per cent litigation goes for trial, the rest are settled out of courts.

However, increase in the number of judges is not the only answer. Some more institutional and systemic reforms are called for. "In India, low levels of remuneration for judges", as pointed out in the Human Development Report in South Asia (1999), "have led to corruption, judicial incompetence, long and drawn-out trials and expensive justice. People are forced to grease the wheels of the system in order to get a quick verdict. According to a 1998 survey, 63 per cent of the respondents reported that they had to bribe court officials in order to get a verdict in their favour. As a result, the vast majority of the Indians feel alienated by the judicial system and learn to live with injustice and violation of their rights."

The Law Commission as well as the National Police Commission in their reports have suggested various measures that can be adopted to reduce the huge backlog of cases in law courts. Some of the immediate steps that can be taken without any delay or difficulty are suggested below:

First, at present, a large number of petty cases, particularly those challaned under different provisions of the Motor Vehicles' Act, form a big bulk of the cases pending in courts for a long period for want of appearance of the accused persons or witnesses who get dispersed in different places after the detection of the offence. There should be ticketing system for on-the-spot disposal of traffic offences which will help in a big way reduction of cases pending for trial in the courts.

Second, Section 320 CrPC provides for compounding of the offences in the courts and prescribes a procedure for it. This compounding can be done only after the police have submitted chargesheets on completion of the investigation. The National Police Commission recommended (Fourth Report) that a quicker disposal of the compoundable cases would be possible if the procedure was altered to enable the police themselves to take note of the desire of the parties to compound the offence even at the stage of investigation and thereupon close the investigation and report the matter to the court, which would pass final orders on the police report. For this some amendment of the Criminal Procedure Code will be necessary. However, this change of procedure will eliminate unnecessary trials of many cases of compoundable nature in law courts.

Third, there should be periodic review at the District level of every police case pending in the court for more than one year from the date of filing of chargesheet and a decision should be taken whether it would be in the public interest to continue with the prosecution or whether the case may be withdrawn. For example, property cases in which the first offenders are involved or cases in which the value of the property is less than Rupees two hundred may be considered for withdrawal with the consent of the complainant. Again, cases involving rioting, ordinary hurt, except those arising from communal clashes, should be considered for withdrawal if the Parties involved in the occurrence agree and the police also feel satisfied that withdrawal will help restoration of amicable relations between the concerned parties. The Law Commission of India in its 154th Report (1996) on the Code of Criminal Procedure 1973 endorsed the recommendation of the National Police Commission and said that "the periodical review of old pending cases can be undertaken with a view to striking them out from the court calendar. It may appear contrary to the principles of natural justice but what is happening in the present situation is not only gross violation of the Directive Principles of the Constitution but a virtual denial of justice. It is a question of choice of the better of two bad options".

Fourth, it is also seen that several cases get adjourned for long periods for securing the presence of the medical officers to give formal evidence in the courts regarding certificates issued by them. As medical officers get transferred from one place to another, very often they do not turn up in courts on the fixed dates resulting in further adjournment of the cases. Section 291 of the CrPC will have to be amended to facilitate acceptance of medical examination reports by medical experts as evidence without insisting on their formal proof by summoning the experts. Similarly, evidence of other experts like chemical examiners, finger-print experts, etc. may be admitted through affidavits.

Fifth, in order to facilitate quick disposal of trials and appeals and alleviate the sufferings of the undertrial prisoners, as recommended by the Law Commission, concept of plea-bargaining should be made acceptable as an experimental measure to offences which are liable for punishment with imprisonment of less than seven years or fine including offences covered by Section 320 of the CrPC. However, plea-bargaining should not be available to habitual offenders accused of social and economic offence of a grave nature and violence against women and children. Plea-bargaining should be made an essential component of the administration of criminal justice. And for this purpose certain guidelines have to be incorporated in the code of criminal procedure.

It is also seen that, at present, witnesses very often do not get in time their daily allowances for appearance in the courts. A sample survey, done by the National Police Commission in 80 magistrates' courts, revealed that out of 96,815 witnesses who attended the courts during the test period, only 6,697 were paid some allowance. It is necessary that the allowance to be paid to the witnesses for their attendance in the court has to be fixed on a realistic basis and the payment should be done through a simple procedure which would avoid delay and inconvenience.

Again, facilities for witnesses in the courts are also hopelessly inconvenient. Witnesses do not want to go to law courts because their attendance in courts entails lot of inconvenience and harassment. I have seen in many rural courts, facilities for drinking water and even chairs and benches for the convenience of the witnesses are not available. As a result, witnesses fight shy of extending a helping hand to the police and only those who have an axe to grind come to help the police.

A vast number of old and outdated laws clutter the statute book. Earlier, a Commission appointed by the Central government concluded that over 1200 central laws were out of date and either needed to be repealed or suitably amended. It is a pity that most of the State governments have not undertaken the exercise to identify laws that have no utility. It has been noticed that punishment prescribed by many laws are so nominal that they have no effect upon the crime situation. It is a waste of time to carry out time-consuming court procedures resulting in a fine of few rupees or simple imprisonment for a few days.

The National Human Rights Commission suggested that enormous burden on criminal courts could be reduced by adopting a system of honorary judicial magistrates on the lines of the institution of Recorders and Assistant Recorders in the United Kingdom. Recorders and Assistant Recorders, who are trained and experienced lawyers, can work part-time on a specific number of days to deal with and dispose of a large number of cases involving minor offences.

In R.D. Upadhyay *Vs* State of Andhra Pradesh, the Supreme Court while emphasising the right to speedy trial guaranteed under Article 21 of the Constitution directed the State government to nominate 10 additional judges to take up exclusively trial and decide long pending cases of murder within a period of six months. Some pilot projects have also been undertaken in some States by utilising the services of retired District and Sessions Judges to preside over the courts where backlog is heavy. Such pilot projects may be adopted for disposal of cases pending for more than two years. There is need for some crash programmes for establishing such courts to deal with old cases to be worked out in each State and put into operation.

Lok Adalats can also play an effective role in expeditious disposal of cases brought before them. Recently, it is reported that the Lok Adalats in Chandigarh cleared 20,000 court cases in 17 months because of the dynamism of Justice S.K. Sardana. There is also lot of scope for improving court management and administration. The judicial administration has, by and large, remained untouched by the management revolution of the 20th century and the information revolution of the present century. Computers can be used successfully in improving the court management. The computers will indicate what cases are related, and related cases could be scheduled on the same date. Effective use of computers in the Supreme Court enabled Justice M.N. Venkatachaliah and Justice Ahmadi to significantly speed up the disposal of old cases.

Again, there is very often untenable and avoidable adjournment of cases both at the stage of trial, appeal and revisions. Though Section 309 of the Criminal Procedure Code provides for holding of the trial proceedings as expeditiously as possible and examination of the witnesses day-to-day, it is an open fact that there is enormous delay in the disposal of cases because of frequent adjournments. Such adjournments, very often, take place on uncertain grounds due to the laxity of the court or the investigating agency. The Law Commission in its 154th Report on "Speedy Justice" recommended that similar measure as laid down under order XVII of the Code of Civil Procedure, introduced by Act 104 of 1976 should be provided. No adjournment shall be granted at the request of a party, except where the circumstances are beyond the control of that party. The Law Commission further recommended the following measures:

> "Every criminal court shall send a return in the prescribed proforma to the Chief Justice of the High Court stating the particulars of the cases in which the adjournments were granted by them during the inquiry or trial of cases detailed reasons therefor."

Today, of the three branches of the State, it is the judiciary that is still held in high esteem by the public. However, the danger to the judicial system is from within. Bad appointments and poor supervision are taking their toll. The criminal justice system is in a shamble and inspires derision, not confidence. The courts occasionally blame the police. The police, in turn, accuse the law and the courts. This game helps no one except defence lawyers and criminals who are happy with the prevailing situations.

3

CORRUPTION TRAP*

The World Bank has defined corruption as the use of "public office for private profit". Corrupt acts include bribery, extortion, embezzlement, use of speed money, etc. Generally, in our country the focus remains on the demand side of corruption and not so much on the supply side. We talk of corruption by the public servants and political leaders forgetting the role of the corrupt businessmen. Corruption is always like two hands clapping

It is an unfortunate fact that with the passage of time corruption level in India has substantially increased. A non-governmental organisation, Transparency International, based in Berlin, has come up with the Corruption Perception Index. It ranks countries according to the level of corruption as assessed by those who do business with the country. Last year, out of 85 countries listed by the Transparency International, India's rank was 66. This year, Transparency International has ranked 99 countries and our rank is 73. Thus, 19 countries were perceived to be more corrupt than India in the last year and this year, 27 countries are considered to be more corrupt. However, this marginal improvement in position should provide no satisfaction. Transparency International has also listed countries in terms of Bribe-payers Perception Index (BPI). The BPI, undertaken by Gallup International for Transparency International in 14 leading market economies, shows that companies from many leading exporting countries regularly resort to bribes for expansion of their business. The BPI reveals that of a scale 0-10, where 10 reads as corruption-free exporting country, the best score among

---

* Appeared in *The Statesman* on 14-2-2001 & 15-2- 2001.

exporting countries was 8.3, while the worst was 3.1. China was seen as having the greatest willingness to pay bribes abroad followed by South Korea, Taiwan, Italy and Malaysia. Sweden, Australia and Canada achieved the most favourable results.

For a developing country like India, corruption is a scourge. It is anti-national. It seriously retards a country's economic development. The UNDP *Report on Human Development in South Asia 1999 — The Crisis of Governance* says that if corruption levels in India were reduced to those of the Scandinavian countries, the investments in the country could increase annually by 10 per cent and GDP growth by almost 1.5 per cent each year. One recent study shows that investing in a relatively corrupt country compared to a relatively honest one is equivalent to additional 15 per cent profit tax on investment. In India, as per the current corruption levels, the implicit corruption tax on investment is almost 20 per cent. Corruption, thus, diminishes the country's capacity for investment by reducing the resources of the government. The high potential for capital flight of illegal earnings makes corruption associated with a very negative impact on the balance of payments.

In India, as well as in many South Asian countries, corruption can be divided into three categories : (a) petty corruption, (b) middling corruption, and (3) grand corruption. There is a growing perception that corruption has moved upwards from petty corruption in 1950s to grand larceny at the highest levels of the State in 1980s and 90s.

Features of Corruption in India

Corruption occurs in almost all countries, but in India and the neighbouring countries of South Asia, corruption has certain characteristic features that make it far more sinister and damaging than corruption in other parts of the world. These features have been highlighted in the UNDP report. First, corruption in India occurs upstream and not downstream. Corruption at the top distorts fundamental decisions about policies, projects and development. In industrialised countries of the West, core decisions are taken through transparent competition and on merit, even though petty corruption may occur downstream. Second, corruption in India has wings and not wheels. Most of the corrupt gains made in the region are immediately smuggled out to safe havens abroad and not ploughed back to domestic production and investments. Third, corruption in India and other Asian countries often leads to promotion and not prison. The big fish are rarely caught. In advanced industrialised countries there is a process of accountability. Even top leaders are not spared. For instance, the former Italian Prime Minister, Bettino Craxy, has been forced to leave in exile in Tunisia to escape extradition due to corruption charges in Rome. The frustrating aspect of the situation in India is corrupt persons are too powerful and beyond accountability. Fourth, corruption in countries like India, where majority of the people live in abject poverty, can have a very unsettling impact. Combating corruption is thus not punishing some dishonest politicians but also saving human lives. Fifth, corruption increases injustice. Basic human rights and freedom are threatened when criminal justice administration is perverted because of misuse of money power. In Bangladesh, in a survey by Transparency International, 90 per cent of the respondents pointed out that the police and judiciary were the most two corrupt institutions. It is a fact that with entrenched corruption the basic trust between citizens and the state disappears. In India also in many courts the people have to offer bribes in order to get a quick verdict. According to a 1998 survey, 63 per cent of the respondents reported that they had to pay bribe to the court officials in order to get a verdict in their favour. Another survey shows that 80 per cent of the people in India feel that they need influence or have to pay bribes in order to see a case through.

Corruption Equation

Robert Klitgaard (Controlling Corruption, Berklay University of California Press) devised a formula that lies at the heart of the corruption problem. It equals corruption with monopoly power plus discretion minus accountability and low government salaries. Corruption takes place when a person has monopoly power over a good or service and has a discretion to decide who will receive it and how much and is not accountable and has a low income level. Thus, the solutions to the problem of corruption need reduction of artificial monopoly power, limited official discretion, increased punishment for the violators and enhanced transparency. Corruption continues because, very often, the offenders feel that they can get away scot-free. In India, most of the government officials know that they would never be caught, and if caught, would escape punishment because of legal delays.

Again, there are some laws and rules in existence, which perpetuate corruption and give opportunities for corrupt practices among the government officials. For instance, it requires 47 different approvals to construct a building in Mumbai and a small-scale entrepreneur has to handle 32 different inspectors and 46 different documents. Malpractices remain unchecked because most of the government departments lack effective in-house vigilance machinery. Many of the government agencies have also developed institutional mechanisms that perpetuate, not eliminate, corruption. Upright officers, who refuse to be corrupted, are frequently transferred to unimportant jobs so that corruption chain is not delinked.

In this connection it may be mentioned that the Santanam Committee on Prevention of Corruption in its report recommended to the government that since corruption was closely related to administrative procedures and abuse of discretion, the Central Vigilance Commission (CVC) which they had proposed to be set up should deal not merely with cases of corruption but also hear complaints against wrong, dilatory or unfair administrative exercises and procedures. The Committee wrote to the then Prime Minister, Lal Bahadur Shastri, that "in order to effectively deal with the problem, it is necessary to take into consideration the root causes, of which the most important is the wide discretionary power which has to be exercised by the executive in carrying on the complicated work of modern administration." However, the Government of India was not in favour of empowering the CVC with the job of looking into the grievances of the citizens against unfair administrative practices and procedures. So, it ordained that the CVC should only look into the matters relating to corruption. It promised that the Department of Administrative Reforms would work out the details of such a machinery. This promise remained unfulfilled. Thus, the CVC could not play the role of ombudsman as in U.K. and other western countries.

Grease-the-Wheel Arrangement

It is argued by some writers that corruption and bribery are necessary lubricants for a cumbersome system of administration. But this "greases the wheel" argument is flawed. Speed money belying the name has the effect of slowing down the pace of administration further. Delay will be deliberately caused in order to invite payments of bribe. This is because of the enormous discretion that many politicians and bureaucrats have over the creation, proliferation and interpretation of counter-productive regulations. Sometimes, it is argued that deregulation or privatisation are the panacea for corruption. This is not a fact. Deregulation and privatisation are not magic wands that can remove corruption overnight. Experience in countries like Russia, China and India have shown that deregulation can lead to an increase in corruption. It is seen that, very often, corrupt rulers may be keen to privatise state assets because of the opportunity for large one-time gains. And again, regulatory powers may be created paradoxically in the process of deregulation. Regulatory Committees set up by the government can be corrupted by the businessmen and monopolists. It is necessary that institutional structure of regulatory agency should be determined before bidding in order to prevent manipulation.

Strategies

It is necessary to devise a series of long-range strategies and short-term measures to deal with the menace of corruption. An anti-corruption revolution, if it is to be credible, must start at the top. To make an impact in public mind, it is necessary to prosecute and punish some major corrupt figures. These are pave-the-path actions necessary to jolt the system out of the corruption trap. Unfortunately, in India till now very few corrupt political leaders or businessmen have been brought to book and hence talk of war against corruption brings cynical reactions from the public.

Actually today, political corruption has become the mother of all kinds of corruption. Hence, some determined action against corrupt politicians is called for. Revision of electoral law is necessary to ensure that anyone chargesheeted or challaned in any criminal case or who has been a history-sheeter in the records of the police should not be given tickets to contest the election.

The National Commission to Review the Working of the Constitution in its paper on the review of "Election Law Processes and Reform Options" has also suggested disqualification of a candidate against whom charges relating to certain crimes have been framed.

Corruption flourishes because punishment is lacking. The conviction rate in India is hardly 6 per cent. Corruption has thus become a low-risk and high-profit activity. The Corrupt Public Servants (Forfeiture of Property) Act, 1999 is pending with the government for consideration since 04.02.1999. It is necessary to pass such an Act so that real punishment by way of confiscation of the property can be enforced.

Politicians, bureaucrats, judges and military officers must be required to make a detailed break-down of their assets position and tax return every year after assuming the office. Actually, if the property statements of the officers are properly scrutinised, action can be initiated against many of the black sheep. Annual Property Returns (APRs) are not submitted, despite clear service rules, by many civil servants regularly. I know of a case where a very senior officer of the rank of Director General of Police did not submit APRs for 15 years and could get away by pleading the ignorance of these rules. If these returns are carefully scrutinised and then followed by swift enquiries against some of the known corrupt public servants living beyond their means, it will have a deterrent impact.

An effective Right to Information Bill would go a long way to help the citizens to combat corruption. In India, the Right to Information Bill is lying in Parliament for several decades. It has still not been passed. It is essential that government policies and programmes become transparent and the people are able to exercise their right to information. The official secrecy code is often used by those in authority to suit their whims. In developed countries like USA, UK and Canada, people have the right to obtain certain documents, except those pertaining to the security of the state and defence matters.

One also notices international double standards in dealing with the corruption problem. There is an urgent need to ensure that all countries should declare bribery illegal, regardless of whether it is paid to foreign officials or national residents. Currently, many European countries have declared bribery illegal when paid to their own nationals, but payment to foreigners are often regarded as necessary for business and are treated as tax deductible payments.

Though corruption has become deeply entrenched, yet it is not impossible to get out of its trap. Countries like France in the 19th century and Singapore and Hong Kong in the 20th century have completed the transition from high-corruption societies to low corruption ones. Strong political will and commitment to a clear anti-corruption agenda can bring about similar outcome in India also. In Hong Kong the Independent Commission against Corruption (ICAC) has done remarkable job in reducing corruption. ICAS was given the power to investigate and prosecute corruption cases and engage in a campaign of public education. The government indicated its commitment by appointing a person of unquestioned integrity to head ICAS and also prosecuting some big fish. In India, highly politicised nature of anti-corruption wings in states shows that very often they have been used for political witch-hunts rather than for catching corrupt officials. Further, lack of real statutory powers have made many of these anti-corruption agencies ineffective.

4

CYBER CRIMES*

Alvin Tofler in his book *Powershift* has pointed out that in the knowledge society, which is now emerging, information will be a commodity of greatest value. Today, the value of a company's future lies not in its tangible assets but in the "intellectual capital of the business". And intellectual capital in most businesses today is kept in the computers. As a consequence, the computer has become the target as well as the instrument for crimes.

From the point of view of a criminal, the web offers anonymity and wonderful opportunities for committing crimes. Criminals transfer funds from the victim's bank account to their own and vandals send computer viruses to destroy other computers. Pedophiles exchange child pornography with others. These offences only represent a few of the crimes which are now committed on the Internet. The perpetrators are men and women from all walks of life and what they need to commit their acts is a computer, and online service and the victim.

Computer crimes can be divided into two general categories: (a) Computers as tool, (b) Computers as target. In the first category of crimes, the computer is used as a tool to commit offences. This group of offenders look upon computer as one of the instruments for committing crimes like fraud, embezzlement and many other related crimes. The second category contains crimes in which the computer itself or the stored information is the target. The criminal groups, who view computers as the targets of crime, have been placed in three categories, (1) hackers, (2) those who break the systems to intentionally cause harm or

---

* Appeared in *The Statesman* on 11-9-2000.

mischief to data or programmes, and (3) financially motivated offenders who use "specialised skill" to steal or damage information contained in the computer storage banks.

Extent of Computer Crimes

The extent of computer crimes is growing rapidly. In 1989, a study by the Florida Department of Law Enforcement, the USA found that 25 per cent of 898 public and private organisations had been victimised. In 1991, United Nations Commission on Crime and Criminal Justice surveyed 3000 sites in Canada, Europe and United States and found that 72 per cent had been victimised.[1]

The fastest growing computer related crime is theft and the most common object stolen is information. Thieves very often target intellectual properties which include things like new product plans, new product descriptions, market programme plans, list of customers and similar information. Previously, thieves obtained such properties by compromising employees, photocopying documents, committing burglaries, but now the *modus operandi* has changed and the thieves would prefer stealing from the computers because it provides extensive access to more useable information.

Cyber Terrorism

Many financial institutions today also receive threats from the cyber terrorists to penetrate their computer systems and leave messages threatening to destroy them unless they receive huge sums of money. Many banks around the world have been victimised and paid millions of dollars as extortion money to keep the system intact. The criminals use various devices that can send a destructive wind through the system. Cyber terrorism is becoming a matter of concern and renders national security systems, banking or communication networks, financial and commercial transactions exposed to great dangers. It is reported that banks, brokering firms and investment houses in the USA, Great Britain and other countries of Europe have secretly paid

1. *FBI Law Enforcement Bulletin* (December, 1996).

huge ransom to prevent costly "computer meltdown" or collapse of confidence among the customers.

Techniques for perpetration of computer crimes have also spawned a new set of terminologies. Some of these are : "Trojan Horse"—a set of unauthorised computer instructions which perform an illegal act at a certain time or under certain conditions, "Trapdoor"—a set of computer instructions that allow the user to bypass the system's normal controls; and "Masquerading"—using a legitimate resource identification number or password to gain access to a computer system.

Cyber Pornography

Another alarming online activity is transmission of child pornography images and making sexual assignation. A study was conducted in 1995 by research team of the Carnegie Mellon University, Pittsburgh, Pennsylvania, titled "Marketing Pornography on the Information Superhighway". It reported that after 18-month research, it found on the Internet 9,17,410 sexually explicit pictures, descriptions, stories and films of naked women, paedophilia, sadomasochism, urination, defecation and sex with animals. Alarmed over cyber pornography, the US Congress enacted Communication Decency Act last year, which prohibited the posting of "indecent" material over the Internet. The Act was, however, overturned by the Supreme Court on grounds of violating freedom of expression.

Risks from the Employees

Analysis of computer crimes suggests that threats of such crimes generally come from the employees. Studies reported on computer crimes have shown that primary threats come from full-time employees, followed by part-time and contract employees, and with computer hackers a close third. There is normally a close correlation between theft and access to computers, but the important thing to recognise is that as networking becomes widespread, access also becomes easier. Today computer hackers with minimal skills can alter the websites. Because of the complexities of certain computer routines and augmented security measures, it is becoming unlikely that one person will possess all the information that is needed to use a computer for criminal purposes. Organised criminal groups, consisting of members from all over the world, have started emerging. Improved telecommunication technology has added to the threat from external sources. International computer criminals use computer-based voicemail box to exchange stolen access numbers, passwords and software. The profile of computer criminals is also interesting. They are bright, sophisticated and technically trained. Increasingly, financial gain is becoming a major motive because many of these professionals live beyond their means. The 'Robinhood' syndrome is also common — they rationalise acts against organisations but believe that acts against individuals are immoral.

Experts on white-collar crimes aver that the chances of computer crimes to be detected are minimal. The computer criminals being sophisticated operators, most of the time their activities do not surface up. The FBI's National Computer Squad, which has investigated the biggest number of crimes estimate that between 85 to 95 per cent of computer intrusions are not even detected. It is also easy for the computer criminals to commit the crime without leaving trace which makes subsequent investigation and prosecution very difficult. So, emphasis should be upon prevention of computer crimes by resolutely following some well-structured crime prevention strategy.

Counter Measures

Data encryption should be considered an important tool for protecting confidential information. However, encryption procedures should be periodically changed and reviewed. Otherwise, breaches of security may occur. Similarly, in respect of cash account security, small account balance errors in computer files should serve as an indicator that somebody has tampered with the accounts. In a rush to commit the crimes the perpetrator is likely to make small rather than large errors. For cash account security, it is necessary to change passwords regularly, operate authentic software, monitor employees and regularly review the cash accounts for small losses.

Firewalls

Firewalls can also be used as a counter-measure. Firewalls are software controls that permit system access only to users, specially registered with the computer. As user attempts to gain access to the system they are challenged to find out if they have authentic passwords. Further, users also encounter other challenges known as layers for greater protection. It has been found that in many cases hackers have penetrated the firewalls. Password-breaker programmes are used by the hackers to beat the security. It is said that when security professionals develop new barriers, hackers approach them like a puzzle rather than an obstacle.

The main responsibility of detecting and investigating cyber crimes in India is that of the police. Unfortunately, they are not trained and equipped properly to discharge it. The first requirement is to familiarise police personnel with various problems of computer crimes. Active co-operation and liaison between the police and software companies will be mutually beneficial. Microsoft in USA trains police officers to combat this sort of crime. Special cells should be established in Police Headquarters, and particularly in the Criminal Investigation Department, in every state to deal with Internet crimes. The cyber space today has become the latest beat of the police. The beat has to be patrolled with high-tech expertise, otherwise, the police will be overtaken by this new form of crime without being able to respond to it properly. It is a fact that, to quote the words of David L. Carter, "Regrettably, the police have fallen behind in the computer age and must overcome a steep learning curve".[2]

In India, specialised investigation units have to be created and staffed with technically qualified investigators to effectively deal with computer frauds as obtaining in FBI (National Computer Crime Squad), Scotland Yard (UK), RCMP (Canada), Netherlands Police, Singapore Police, and so on. A proposal has been made for establishing a Computer Investigation Group in the CBI.

---

2. David L. Carter, "Computer Crime Categories—How Techno-Criminals Operate", *FBI Law Enforcement Bulletin*, July 1995.

In the investigation of computer crimes a team-approach is necessary. Ideally, a team should comprise an investigator, a computer expert and an EDP auditor. Investigations frequently require search of a computer centre or a remote computer terminal. The assistance of a data processing expert becomes necessary to draft search warrants which include all pertinent systems and programme components. A high level of secrecy during investigation has to be maintained so as not to alert the suspected perpetrator. This is most important because within seconds the suspect can erase or damage such evidence as data and programmes.

Problems Faced by the Investigators

Successful investigation of computer crimes requires high degree of computer literacy on the part of the investigators. Most of the evidence of computer crimes will be in the form of electronic data. Hence, its search, seizure and preservation would require good computer knowledge on the part of the investigators. The investigating officer must also know file directory management and information recovery i.e. undeleting supposedly deleted files and information or viewing hidden files. Training of the investigators must also cover overcoming passwords, comprehending and investigating financial crimes. Importantly, most of the computer crimes are not limited to the territory of a particular country. This creates serious problems during investigation and prosecution of computer crimes. Different laws in different countries make some kind of behaviour legal in one country and illegal in another. Extradition and prosecution issue also creates problems.

In USA in 1996, the National Information Infrastructure Protection Act was passed. The new statute provides that individuals, who access protected computers without authority, will be responsible for the consequences of their account and those access with authority are criminally liable only if they intend to cause damage to the victim. In India, IT Act, 2000 has come into effect from 1st June, 2000. India is one of the few countries which has enacted such an Act to facilitate e-commerce and to deal with the perpetrators of cyber crimes. Cyber crime is a new form of crime and it is going to escalate in the coming years. Concerted efforts are required on the part of the investigators to prepare themselves in advance before this kind of crime assumes gigantic proportions.

5

COMMUNITY POLICING*

Community policing has become the buzzword of law enforcement across the world. However, practices which are defined as community policing vary widely. David H. Bayley writes in *Police for Future*, "Because the phrase has so often been used imprecisely, it has been cheapened. one police chief thought that any contact between police and public was community policing and another chief of detectives said that criminal investigation is the epitome of community policing". In reality, community policing implies changing the conception of the role of the police in society. Community policing refers to arrangements for policing that accord a significant role to "the community" in defining and guiding policing in their locality. Key elements of community policing included community crime prevention, active solicitation by police of requests for public service and the provision of opportunities for feedback from the communities about police operations.

A survey of community policing in the USA and some of the countries of Western Europe goes to show that the period of 1960s and 1970s saw the dawn of the "Professional policing model" to replace the "Beat cop" who knew the residents of the locality where he was assigned to perform duties. A central element of the professional bureaucratic model of policing, that emerged, was the use of most up-to-date technology in police work and insulation of the police from political influence. However, it became clear gradually that professional policing model possessed its own innate shortcomings. Technological

---

* Appeared in *The Statesman* on 7-6-2000 & 8-6-2000.

advances were reducing police contacts with the public as the police spent more time in high-tech equipped cars. Officers were losing touch with the communities they were meant to serve. Further, this model also did not help prevention of rise in crimes. especially in the inner cities. Community policing emerged in 1970s and 1980s as the police recognised that their tactics were not able to reduce crimes and were in some cases contributing to civil disturbances. Officers involved in community related policing develop access to the residents on a personal level which help them to build a better relationship between the community and the police. The community becomes more involved with the police and serves as its "eyes and ears" in the neighbourhood. The central theme of community policing is that the public should play a more active role in promoting public safety. The police cannot bear the responsibility alone. The public should be seen as co-producers with the police of safety and order.

Key Features

Therefore, if community policing is to mean anything distinctive, it must refer to programmes that change the interaction between the police and the public. A full-fledged community policing programme incorporates the following :

1. Community-based crime prevention;
2. Decentralized command;
3. Increased accountability to the local communities; and
4. Re-orientation of patrol activities to render non-emergency services.

Though community policing is first and foremost a crime prevention effort, it does not mean cessation of police efforts to detect crime and arrest and prosecute the offenders. Investigative policing has to continue side by side with the community policing. Successful community policing can improve and enhance other police operations by increasing community's cooperation with the police.

There is facile assumption that community policing assumes that the public wants partnership with the police. Very often this is not the case. There is community's sceptism and a feeling that they have all heard it before. There is also fear of the public that they will face reprisals from the criminals if they cooperate with the police. To win community's confidence and trust, the police have to demonstrate that they sincerely seek community's help in combating crime and disorder. It has also been noticed that community policing is more successful in well-organised and cohesive communities which need community policing least. It is difficult to mobilise support in disorganised communities separated by caste, creed and religious divisions.

Community-oriented policing, points out Dr. David Bayley in his article "The Best Defence", breaks down the anonymity of policing and diminishes the psychological distance between the police and the public. It puts faces into uniforms and allows the community to know the police in human terms. It is a fact that most of the citizens are not opposed to law enforcement but resent partisan law enforcement. They want an assurance that enforcement is justified in particular circumstances. Community policing transforms the police officers from being agents of law to the upholders of the community values. It has to be kept in mind that police action should not be guided and influenced exclusively by community norms. Police officers have obligations to enforce the laws without fear or favour, even if the communities fail to understand them. However, community policing gives the police an opportunity to take action keeping in mind the community norms. Further, community policing also minimizes over-reaction. But getting to know the communities well, the police are less likely to over-react in their encounters with the public. Very often, is police over-reaction that triggers communal violence and riots. Knowledge of a community reduces the fear of dealing with the community in unfamiliar conditions. It also goes to enhance the police responsiveness.

Singapore Experience

To make community policing effective and successful the police have to take some important operational measures. First, in each police station there should be community police officers to establish contacts with the people from all walks of life in the neighbourhood. The police should set up neighbourhood committees to consult the citizens about their local problems and priorities. Community police officers should make themselves available for frequent non-emergency meetings with the citizens. In Singapore, as an important strategy for fighting and preventing crime the police have set up a number of Neighbourhood Police Centres (NPCs). The NPC officers conduct house visits on a regular basis to disseminate crime prevention advice and to obtain feedback on the community needs. They work closely with the community and grassroots organisations such as Citizens' Consultative Committees (CCCs) and Community Development Councils (CDCs) to address the community's safety and security concerns. The introduction of the NPCs is a part of the restructuring of the Singapore Police Force (SPF) to meet the policing challenges of the 21st century. Successful working of the NPCs has enabled the Singapore Police to provide better and more efficient services to the community. There is greater community focus and overall enhancement and improvement of police-community relations.

Consultation with the communities for crime prevention and control is now happening in many democratic countries. Britain has established over 200 Community Consultative Committees at the precinct level. These Consultative Committees often enable the police to know of the local needs and problems. The police often find to their surprise that the people are concerned not only with serious crimes like rape, murder and robbery, which are publicised in the media, but also with the recurrent low-key troubles. Some of the issues can be settled quickly by the police with the citizens' cooperation. These meetings also enable the members of the community to ventilate their grievances against the police and criticise openly the police officers for their acts of omission and commission. I attended such a meeting in Birmingham during my visit to the U.K. in 1997. The meeting gave opportunities to the citizens to ventilate their grievances against the police and the police in their turn tried to explain the steps that they have taken and intended to take in future in respect of various issues raised by the members of the public. The information provided by the police also enable the citizens to refine their operations.

It is true that community-oriented policing does not transform police officers into social workers. It does, however, empower officers to connect individuals with problems to agencies that can help them. It recognises the value of the police and the community working together to reduce crime. Such a relationship, as one American police officer says, is a "win-win situation".

However, there are problems. The most serious impediment to the community policing programmes is often police resistance. This often spurs from police resistance to innovative changes and practices, and a threat to police autonomy. There is also the lurking fear that it may politicise public security functions. Further, meaningful community policing implies that the police must be prepared to change in response to the views of the community. Community policing implies not only some change of procedures but a long-time reform process that seeks to change the institutional culture of the police over time.

Police unions internationally view community policing as a threat to police professionalism. They feel that police are the appropriately trained agency to control crime and in this work the citizens are neither needed nor wanted. Further, community policing also requires some kind of police accountability to the community, and this is not acceptable to the police unions who further fear loss of jobs and benefits. It is also a fact that sometimes many citizens come to believe that community policing interferes with the standard of crime-fighting and demand a return to the traditional methods of policing. Obstacles also come from police sub-culture where display of authoritarian use of force is appreciated. Police officers become tough and skeptical of innovation. In community policing, however, the police have to play a problem-solving parental role.

Evaluation

Evaluating crime prevention strategies such as community policing is more complex than traditional assessments of law enforcement.

It has to rely on the outcome of the programme and cannot be based on the qualitative analysis of the process. Indeed, in some cases, the number of crimes reported to the police has increased after introduction of the community policing programmes as a result of enhanced community-police dialogue and trust. Indeed, expectations of community policing should be realistic. These programmes may produce marginal reduction in crime, but diminish the citizens' fear and improve their attitudes towards the police.

It can be mentioned in this connection that in the USA a major comparative evaluation conducted by the University of Maryland found that "there is no evidence that Community Policing *per se* reduces crime without a clear focus on crime risk factor objective." The same study, however, goes on to conclude that "patrols and programmes directed on crimogenic substances like guns and alcohols can be effective in attacking crimes hotspots". Indeed, in some cases the number of crimes reported to the police has increased following introduction of community policing as a result of enhanced public trust and confidence, though it may give the statistical appearance of a rise in crime.

Unfortunately, there is no in-built mechanism for community policing within our police system and structure. Some sincere and well-meaning police chiefs have experimented with community policing programmes with some degree of success. Shri Vijay Karan as the Commissioner of Police, Delhi in 1989 and recently the Commissioner of Police, Bangalore took a number of initiatives to involve the community in different crime prevention and law enforcement programmes. But these efforts by enlightened and enthusiastic police chiefs have been somewhat sporadic and impermanent. The community policing system has not been sincerely and seriously tried in our country. I recently attended a seminar in Bangalore where the city Police Chief mentioned about the various community policing initiatives taken by them. Different NGO groups also lauded the police role. However, it could be seen that no evaluation of the programmes, that have been launched so far, has been made. As a result, changes and modifications of the programmes in the light of the evaluations have not taken place.

6

KILLED IN LINE OF DUTY*

Reports of the killings of policemen appear in newspapers with disturbing regularity. They do not seriously perturb public mind and only evoke occasional sighs of sympathy. Death of a policeman in line of duty is viewed with shock and horror in many developed countries because a policeman is viewed as a symbol of the authority of the government. His death in the hands of the criminals is looked upon as a challenge to the state power and bestirs public conscience. Unfortunately, in India killing of a policeman does not produce the sense of shock and outrage which one notices in countries like the U.K. or Japan. This happens because policemen in line of duty are killed so often that emotion gets blunted by familiarity. Killing of a policeman is accepted as an occupational hazard. The number of police fatalities has sharply increased with eruptions of terrorist violence in different parts of the country. 626 police personnel were killed on duty in 1996, 597 in 1997, and 638 in 1998. Of the 638 policemen killed on duty in 1998, 53 were gazetted officers, 517 lower subordinates (constables and head constables and 68 upper subordinates (sub-inspectors and inspectors).

Well trained and heavily armed terrorist outfits are launching surprise attacks on police posts or Policemen on duty in Jammu and Kashmir, North East and other parts of the country and inflicting heavy casualties. They are making good use of the lethal weapons in their armoury. Indeed, easy availability of guns and explosives and their miniaturisation has provided deadly fire, power to the terrorists. Induction of well-trained fanatical foreign

---

* Appeared in *The Statesman* on 13-5-2001.

mercenaries in Jammu and Kashmir has further compounded the situation.

No doubt, increasing incidents of fatal attacks have an unsettling impact on the morale and outlook of policemen in many ways. First, it creates among the police officers and men a seize mentality. Deprived of solicitude from the members of the public, the police feel that they have to strike hard against their enemies, and it is not possible to follow the rules of the game. They also develop a high degree of occupational solidarity bolstered by a feeling that in crisis situations, no policemen can count on help from others except the police; they are alone to stand or fall together. Second, such incidents provoke virulent police aggression. I remember an occasion long ago when I was posted as the Deputy Inspector General of Police in Rourkela in Western Orissa. A constable on night patrol duty was murdered by some criminals, when he challenged them on the road. Almost a blind fury gripped officers and men, and it was very difficult for the senior officers to restrain them from applying rough and ready justice to the criminals when the latter were apprehended. The policemen display on such occasions a very high degree of occupational solidarity, bolstered by a feeling that the people in general are hostile to the police.

Third, a strong feeling grows up within the police that those who attack the police must get their comeuppance. They adopt ruthless and illegal counter measures, particularly while dealing with the dreaded criminals and terrorists. And the members of the public also back them. Fourth, there is demand for sophisticated and effective weaponry. During the terrorist violence in the Punjab, it was argued that the police with their old 303 rifles were in no position to face the deadly fire-power of the terrorists equipped with quick firing automatic rifles. The fact is forgotten that it is neither possible nor desirable to heavily arm all police posts. Apart from the risks of misuse and loss of weapons, this step will further alienate the police from the public.

In this connection it may be mentioned that in the U.S.A. also police officers run the high risk of being murdered or seriously injured on the job. The risk of being murdered for an

American police officer in the 1980s was 22 per 1,00,000 annually as compared to 1.4 for police in England and Wales. David Lester in his study of the "Officers' attitudes towards police use of force in the U.S.S." concluded that the states where police officers were murdered at a higher rate were also those states where civilians murdered one another at a higher rate and where police officers killed the civilians as a higher rate. In other words, police officers in violent areas tend to behave more violently. Thus, working in a community where murder is common would also affect police attitudes towards the use of force. It is also a fact that sometimes police officers feel that community is more hostile to them. Crawford in his study of 'Police overperception of ghetto hostility' found the evidence that some more prejudiced and less educated officers were specially prone to overestimate the hostility towards the police in the city.

Again, expectation of serious dangers on the job have its impact on the attitude and outlook of the police officers. It is found that policemen, who have had greater expectations of facing dangers, were less inclined to help the civilians in their daily encounters. Further, for the police in democratic societies there is always the need to build up an organisational culture that frowns on misuse and abuse of force. It becomes difficult to develop that kind of organisational ethos and culture when large number of policemen get feloniously killed in the line of duty. Another unsavoury fallout is encouragement of police vigilantism.

On the subject of attacks on the police very little empirical study has been done in our country. However, the Bureau of Police Research and Development in its study (1990) of police fatalities in India found that out of a total number of 10,000 police personnel, who were killed in line of duty, during the period between 1983 to 1987, 77 per cent of the casualties occurred in the ranks of upper subordinates and the maximum number of police personnel who were killed in the line of duty were between the age group of 31 to 35 years. Thus, a significantly high number of police personnel lost their lives at a young age. This also reflects the courage, dedication to duty and the sacrifice made by the police. The study also revealed increasing number of policemen getting killed in accidents. As many as 1896 policemen lost their lives in accidents in the country during this period. Vehicle accident, drowning accidents and accidents involving use of fire firearms and explosives claimed the largest number of police lives. The study suggested the need for reviewing the training programmes for developing self-protection awareness among the police personnel.

In this connection it may be mentioned that Prof. Harman Conardie of the Department of Criminology of South Africa made an analytical study of reasons behind killings of policemen in South Africa. In South Africa more than 200 policemen had been killed each year since 1993. Before democratic elections in 1994, the informed view of the social scientists was that these killings took place because the police were perceived as the most oppressive arm of the apartheid regime and hence looked down upon as the enemies of the people. But even after the installation of the democratic government, there was no abatement of the killings of the police officials. Prof. Conradie interviewed a number of prisoners who had been found guilty by the court of law for murdering police officials. The research results indicated that the dominant motive behind the police killings was to escape arrest. Prof. Conradie's study confirmed the earlier findings of Margarita Mona 1980 (Killing the Police—Myths and Motives), who studied police killings in the USA and determined five motives. The motives were perseverance in violence, defence of personal autonomy, protection against concrete danger, defence or protection of others and as an expression of contempt. The study also showed that if police officials were careful and maintained the strategic distance during confrontation with the subjects, risks of attacks on them could be minimised.

Kiselhorst identified (A theoretical perspective of violence against the police) a number of factors regarding the police officers' manner of interaction that may cause the officer to be assaulted — lack of competence, errors in judgement, negative attitudes and prejudices. Too often, police officers betray errors in judgement and make careless mistakes resulting in their deaths or injuries. They misjudge a situation and fail to follow prescribed safety regulations. Finally, an officer with a prejudicial attitude increases the possibility of becoming a victim of violence.

Preventive Measures

Some specific preventive measures can be taken to ensure greater safety for the police officers. One is to improve training. There should be constant training to provide police with skills they need to deal with sudden assaults on them. Very often officers lose their lives for carelessness and complacency. Effective career-long training remains the best protection for always vulnerable police officers. Again, with the expansion of technology, different kinds of protective garments for the police have been devised. In this respect soft body armour has been a major breakthrough. It has been responsible for saving the lives of many police officers.

The FBI annual reports on law enforcement officers killed or assaulted document the felonious slaying of 1845 officers during the years 1972-91. It showed how without soft body armour the death toll of the American police slain feloniously during the 20-year period would have been more than 2600. Initially, there were body armour made of silk fibres which provided limited protection against handgun bullets fired at low velocity. The major breakthrough has come with introduction of vest made of strong plastic fibre garment made by Dupont. The vest protects by catching the bullet in a netline web of fibres and the fibres elongate in response to the collision and absorb the energy of the bullet. The police in various American cities are now wearing bullet proof vests that had earlier been left lying in the lockers.

7

POLICE ACCOUNTABILITY AND CIVILIAN OVERSIGHT

Accountability means answerability for the proper performance of the assigned job. It means, as emphasised by the National Police Commission in its report (Eighth Report of the National Police Commission, page 1), more than mere responsibility to discharge the duties involved in a job, but includes the responsibility of doing so in a manner to the satisfaction of the party for whose benefit the responsibilities are being discharged. In a democratic society, the police remains ultimately accountable for its performance to the people. It has also a proximate responsibility to the law of the land which in essence expresses the will of the people. In every stage of their activity the police should be governed and judged by the provisions of law. Protection of the basic rights of the people and compliance with law are the twin pillars of good policing in a liberal democratic society. The relationship of the police to law is, therefore, instrumental as well as professional. It is a tool in their hands for initiating action against the law-breaking members of the community, it also defines the standards of performance by the police themselves in the execution of their public duties.

Law gives powers to the police to exercise force for the purpose of peace-keeping. Indeed, the mandate of the police to use force to curb greater violence and disorder raises the key issue that the police themselves should not indulge in abuse or misuse of force. Exercise of police powers must be subjected to checks and balances. Indeed, no state body with the possible exception of the armed forces stand on a routine basis between the protection and endangerment of human rights.

However, checks and balances on police power, if they are to serve the intended purposes, must be reliable as well as effective in their nature and operation. They must also be perceived as such by the members of the community.

Checks and regulations of police misconduct can be internal as well as external. Many senior police officers as well as experts like David Bayley feel that internal control is to be preferred to the external processes. Bayley has argued in his book, *Pattern of Policing—A Comparative International Analysis*, that internal regulation can be more thorough, effective and efficient than external supervision. A determined police can hide many things from external supervision and can make it haphazard and ineffective. However, external control is needed whenever it is felt that the police force on its own cannot control itself internally. Experience of dealing with police misconduct in different parts of the world shows that exclusive reliance on police self-regulation may not be sufficient. Capacity of the police to regulate itself is limited. And further police self-regulation, howsoever well-meaning, does not carry conviction with the people. And that is the reason why civilian oversight of the police has emerged as one of the legitimate means by state authorities to exercise checks on police powers. Public demand for civilian oversight has acquired edge because of the widely held perception that police supervisors often tend to gloss over the misdeeds of their subordinate staff.

Turning to the evolution of civilian oversight bodies in democratic countries, it is seen that the 1980s represented, to quote Dr. David Bayley, "a watershed period with respect to the moral dimension of policing". During those years civilian review bodies were created in many countries. In sum, the police lost their monopoly in determining whether the police officers were treating their citizens right.

Object

The record of experience with civilian oversight in various forms indicates that some important considerations have to be kept in mind if the system is to operate successfully and effectively. It has to be kept in mind that the goal is not primarily the punishment of the police but the goal is to restore public confidence in the police as well as to ensure police compliance with rules and regulations. There is very little point in talking in terms of only punishing the aberrant officers unless there are efforts for systemic changes and efforts in the police to persuade the officers, particularly street-level officers, of the need to change existing practices.

Independent Investigative Capacity

Any civilian oversight body in order to be effective should have an independent investigative capacity. If an independent investigation can be launched from the moment a serious complaint is received, it will reassure the citizens who may otherwise feel that the police may seek to cover up serious transgressions. However, independent investigation should be taken up only in respect of very important cases. Other cases should be dealt by mediation, conciliation and internal police investigation. In the investigation set-up there must not only be police officers or ex-police officers, but investigators with different backgrounds like lawyers, academics and doctors, who cannot be charged with pro-police sympathies. This does not mean that the police investigators are to be excluded. The Australian Law Reforms Commission stated in its report that in complaints which involve serious criminal charges, investigation can be carried out best by experienced police personnel.

Civilian oversight has offered a separate means by which grievances can be made against the police, and investigation can be monitored and conducted by independent investigators and some independent assessment can be made of the results of the investigation. The crucial element here is the induction of a third non-police party in the resolution of the grievances against the police, and it offers fresh and new ways of resolving these grievances. Further, a functional complaints system enables the socially weak and marginalised groups to articulate their grievances. It thus gives an opportunity to the common citizens to influence the course of police policy, procedures and practices. It can foster community policing by including the genuine grievances of those citizens who are removed from society's institutions.

Resistance

Experience in different countries shows that attempts to set up civilian oversight mechanisms have met with stiff police opposition and resistance. There is always police opposition stemming from the perceived threat to police professionalism and also from the feeling that jurisdiction over the discipline of the members of the police force belongs "exclusively to the command structure". Police unions in countries like the United Kingdom, Canada and Australia have argued that the lay involvement would result in a lack of appreciation of the police work and the problems faced by the police including the occupational hazards of vindictive and vexatious complaints. In the United Kingdom when the Police Complaints Board (PCB) was established by the Police Act of 1976, Sir Robert Mark, the well-known Commissioner of London Metropolitan Police resigned in protest. In Victoria (Australia) the Police Complaints Authority, which was set up in July 1986, had to face strong opposition from the Police Association which sought an injunction from the Supreme Court in Australia to prevent the Authority from initiating enquiries in relation to the police conduct. The Australian Supreme Court in the wellknown case (Servy *Vs* McCrohan) overruled the objection. The government, however sided with the police, and abolished the Police Complaints Authority in 1989 and replaced it by ombudsman to oversee police internal investigation into the complaints.

In Canada, the Metropolitan Toronto Police Force Complaints Act, 1984, set up in Toronto the Civilian Board of Enquiry comprising members appointed from amongst the distinguished citizens and police officers who must not be either serving police officers or nominated by the Police Association. The Police Association challenged the validity of the Metropolitan Toronto Police Act and went to the extent of partial withdrawal from service demanding the repeal of the Act. In Canada, the police officers tried to criticize the Civilian Review Board as 'Kangaroo

Courts' in which the few basic rights of the police officers and investigators were honoured. While the merits of some of these criticisms can be questioned, they go to indicate the type of opposition that is encountered by the external review mechanisms. For its own success it is necessary for the outside agency to strive sincerely and continually to persuade the police to understand the wider implications of proper handling of the complaints and make them realise that in their own interest they should consider review by external mechanisms as beneficial. Indeed, willing compliance is always preferable to exacted deterrence. The Metropolitan Toronto Police Act, 1984 was repealed. A new Police Service Act, 1989 was enacted which expanded the jurisdiction of the Public Complaints Commissioner on a mandatory basis throughout the province. The Toronto complaints system had been the catalyst for civilianisation of the police complaints procedures throughout Canada. The Royal Canadian Mounted Police amended its Act to create a Public Complaints Commission to provide transparency in the investigation of allegations of misconduct on the part of the members of the RCMP.

Despite initial opposition police leaders in many countries have gradually veered round to the view that civilian control mechanism ultimately helps the police in many ways. It helps the police managers to improve service delivery by identifying the weaknesses in their programmes and take steps to be more responsive to the expectations of the communities. This is particularly important in, to quote the Chief of Royal Canadian Mounted Police, J.P.R. Murray, a "demand-driven" organisation like the police. Civilian oversight can also identify policies, guidelines and regulations and even legislative requirements which may be contributing factors in events leading to public complaints against the police.

However, functioning of Civilian Review bodies has not always been acclaimed by the complainants themselves. In a major study evaluating the work done by the Police Complaints Authority in the UK, Maguire and Corbett pointed out that the system failed to command public confidence because in most of the cases allegations against the police remained unsubstantiated. Substantiation rate has always appeared to the outsiders far too low to constitute an effective deterrent. This happens because obtaining evidence against the malpractice of the police is difficult. Very often, malpractice occurs in police territory and the police officers who break the law always have the opportunity to hide the misconduct from the civilian witnesses. There is also a code of silence among the police officers. Maguire study also showed that some of the complainants were making their first complaints against the police in their lives and "felt that it is like walking upto a six-feet man". They expected some kind of relief or an assurance that steps would be taken to prevent such recurrence.

Why Police Resort to Shortcut Methods?

Now the question arises as to why the police resort to shortcut and illegal methods in the performance of their duties. Maurice Punch in a perceptive study called "Conduct Unbecoming" has stated that the roots of police deviance are deep-seated and multi-dimensional. Its stems from, as seen in various countries of the world, ambiguous legislation, vulnerability to legal sanctions, occupational culture and a desire to produce quick results. In countries like India, the public expect the police to take laws in their hands because of the working of the criminal justice system at a snail's pace. There is demand for ruthless counter-measures in spite of the price to be paid in terms of human rights. It is the responsibility of the police leaders to resist such pressures and check drifts of this kind. They have to keep in mind that in any democratic society order maintained by repression is the worst form of disorder. It establishes a linkage between social order and atrocity.

National Human Rights Commission

In India, the National Human Rights Commission since its inception has been receiving a large number of complaints against the police. Some of the complaints have been found to be frivolous but there is substance in many of the complaints. In a number of cases the Commission has awarded compensation to the victims and suggested disciplinary action against the errant police officers. The Commission, however, has strongly felt that punishment or disciplinary action against the errant police officials will not be adequate unless there is a systemic change. For this purpose, the Commission strongly recommended the insulation of the police from extraneous pressure and influence. In its submission before the Supreme Court in the Writ Petition (Writ Petition No. 310 of 1996, Prakash Singh and others *Vs* Union of India), the Commission referred to the doctrine of constabulary independence in the U.K. and endorsed the observations of the Royal Commission of Police, 1962 and Lord Denning regarding constables' responsibility and answerability to law alone. The Commission referred to the observation of Sir Robert Mark, a well-known Commissioner of London Metropolitan Police, that the police in Great Britain is answerable to law and this makes them "the least powerful, the most accountable and the most acceptable police in the world". Police in democratic society should be low in authority and high in accountability. The Commission also endorsed the recommendation of the National Police Commission for the constitution of a State Security Commission to oversee police work and insulate the police from unnecessary and avoidable interference.

The State Security Commission will have representatives from cross-sections of the society and the accountability of the police to the people will be brought through this mechanism. Further, accountability will be ensured when people become aware of their rights and are willing to exercise them through available mechanisms and agencies. Awareness does not mean only awareness of rights but also awareness of the problems and constraints within which the police have to function.

The National Human Rights Commission further pointed out in its submission before the Apex Court that altogether the "rule of law in modern India, the frame upon which justice hangs, has been undermined by the rule of politics. Supervision in the name of democracy has eroded the foundations on which impartiality depends in the criminal justice system". For better accountability of the police, the Commission suggested the formation of District

Complaints Authority to examine complaints from the public of police excesses, arbitrary arrests and detentions and make recommendations to the government and the State or National Human Rights Commission and institution of lay-visitors for visiting jails and police lock-ups.

In the ultimate analysis, essential features of democratic policing are responsiveness and accountability. A democratic police force, to quote Dr. Bayley, "responds the needs of individuals and private groups as well as the needs of the government. It is accountable to multiple audience and multiple mechanisms". Strengthening of these mechanisms will strengthen the quality of democratic policing.

SECTION - II

8

TRAFFICKING OF WOMEN AND CHILDREN*

Trafficking of women and children is one of the worst violations of human rights. It is a matter of great shame that even after half a century since the adoption of the Universal Declaration of Human Rights by the international community, trafficking continues to thrive. The International Organisation for Migration (IOM) estimates that global trafficking industry generates upto eight billions of U.S. dollars each year from what may be described as 'trade in human misery'.

There are many forms of trafficking. But the most visible and widespread is the trafficking of women and children for commercial exploitation. This kind of exploitation of women and children is not a new phenomenon. Its origin goes to the history and traditions of many countries. However, the problem has now been exacerbated by globalisation and its linkage with lucrative tourist and sex industries. Though it is a global phenomenon, the problem has assumed alarming dimensions in different countries of Asia, and particularly South Asia.

At present, there is no single clear-cut definition of trafficking. The term is used to describe activities that range from voluntary migration to the movements of persons through force, or violence for exploitative purposes. The 'U.N. Special Rapporteur on Violence Against Women'–Radhika Coomaraswamy has correctly pointed out that at the core of any definition of trafficking, must be recognition of the fact that trafficking is never consensual. It is this non-consensual nature of trafficking that distinguishes

---

* Appeared in *The Statesman* on 31-3-2001.

it from other forms of migrations. Thus, all kinds of illegal migration are not trafficking and the basic distinction between the two is the question of consent.

Today, South Asia has emerged alongside South-East Asia as a major centre for intra and international trafficking of women and children. Trafficking of women is done primarily for the purposes of prostitution, but also for use as bonded labourers, beggars and smugglers. Major international flows include trafficking of girls from Nepal and Bangladesh to India and from Bangladesh and Burma to Pakistan and from Pakistan and India to the Middle East. Further, trafficking of young boys from India and Pakistan to the Middle East for use as camel-jockies has also assumed alarming proportions. Though there is dearth of hard accurate data, the fact remains that this volume of trafficking of women and children in India is disproportionately high.

Trafficked women and children are used for varieties of purposes like prostitution, domestic work, camel jockies, illegal adoption of children, organ transplant, begging, drug-trafficking, forced marriages and various other exploitative forms of work. Both demand and supply factors ruthlessly drive the trafficking industry. Some key push factors are inadequate employment opportunities, lack of social safety net, globalisation, relaxed control and open border facilitating movement of population. Other important contributing factors are–erosion of traditional family system as well as values, the pursuit of consumerism and traditional practices in some communities like dedicating girls to gods and goddesses. Further, social acceptance of prostitution in some communities encourages the clandestine trade.

Nepal today is the largest identifiable source of child prostitutes to Indian brothels. UNICEF Review indicates that from five thousand to seven thousand girls are trafficked to India every year. The UNICEF survey mentioned that Nepali girls and young virgins sell for atleast six thousand rupees each in Indian brothels on their first nights. Virgins are prized because of the prevalent myth that sleeping with the virgins will cure sexually transmitted diseases. Fear of AIDS also has raised the demand for the virgins. Traffickers manipulate Nepal's poor economic condition to their advantage. Families from poor communities in Nepal, who are in dire economic straits, becomes easy victims of the traffickers who offer them either job or proposals for marriage. Bombay has the largest number of Nepalese girls in prostitution. According to one estimate, there are about 20,000 Nepali women in the city's flesh trade. Many of them hail from remote hilly villages and poor communities of Nepal. They were brought by the local recruiters and then sold off to the brokers, who delivered them to the brothel owners in India. Out of them, 60 per cent contract HIV. Because Nepali women and girls in brothels are trapped in virtual slavery, they are unable to negotiate any aspect of the situation. Information on AIDS is admittedly of limited practical use. Nevertheless, it is one of their only remaining lines of defence against contracting and transmitting AIDS virus. AIDS education for Nepali women will help them to assert some control over their lives by informing their decisions about marriage and children if they return to their home villages. According to another survey done by Dasgupta, Bangladeshi girls and women constitute almost 11 per cent of the total number of prostitutes in Calcutta. Difficult economic condition in Bangladesh and oppression and torture of the girls by their husbands are some of the causative factors. Many of the prostitutes of the brothels in Calcutta are poor Muslim girls who have been picked up by the traffickers by promising marriage and employment. Some of them with children have been abandoned by their husbands and in desperate need to support their children are left with no alternatives but to enter the profession.

In a study of the sexual exploitation of the Nepalese girls, Durga Ghcmiri, a well-known social worker of Nepal, points out that young girls are often deceived by pimps or middle persons who offer them jobs in urban areas. There are also a large number of step-mothers and step-fathers, who sell their girls to the brothel owners. There are many professional husbands as well who marry the girls and sell them to the brothel owners. Last year, she was able to recover 124 minor girls working as prostitutes in Bombay. The girls in sex industries face intimidation, rape and torture from the pimps, clients, brothel owners and even the law-enforcement agents. There is very often coercion and physical abuse.

Constitutional and Legal Aspects

Article 23 of Part III of the Indian Constitution related to fundamental rights under the caption 'Rights Against Exploitation" prohibits trafficking of the human beings and provides that any contravention of this right shall be an offence punishable by law. The Directive Principles of State Policy under Part IV of the Constitution in Article 39 (e) and (k) declare that state policies should be directed towards securing that the "childhood and youth are protected against exploitation and material abandonment."

Building on the constitutional principles the Suppression of Immoral Traffic in Women and Girls Act was enacted in 1956. The Act was amended in 1986 and ratified as the Immoral Traffic (Prevention) Act. The amended Act continues to prohibit prostitution in its commercialised form without making prostitution *per se* an offence. The Act prescribes stringent action against those procuring children for the purpose of prostitution. If the offence is committed against a child, the punishment is rigorous imprisonment for a term not less than seven years. Regrettably, enforcement of the Act by the State governments has been extremely poor. Cases of clandestine inter-State and cross- border trafficking in women and girls are seldom thoroughly investigated. Consequently, the basic structure of the cruel and exploitative system remains intact and continues to flourish. Section 13 (4) of the Act empowers the central government to appoint trafficking police officers with nation-wide jurisdiction for the investigation of cases of inter-State trafficking in women. No step has so far been taken by the government in this regard to appoint 'Trafficking Police Officers'. A central investigation agency, notably the Central Bureau of Investigation, should be directed by the government to perform the functions of 'trafficking officers' as envisaged under the provisions of the Act.

Again, under Section 13 of the Act the State governments are to appoint special police officers who should be assisted by an advisory body comprising leading social welfare workers of the area. This, if done, will create a mechanism at the field level to initiate and sustain appropriate action. Indeed, effective implementation of the provisions of the IPTA needs far greater police vigilance. It is the police collusion which often enables the pimps and traffickers to operate without fear and get away scot-free. Moreover, cross–border trade in women and children is not possible without the connivance of the police and the personnel of the Border Security Force.

Regional Co-operation

There is also need for regional co-operation for combating effectively this menace of trafficking in women and children. Recently (22nd October, 2000), a regional workshop of senior police officers to enhance cross-border collaboration to stop human trafficking was held in Kathmandu. A body of professionals called 'South Asia Professionals Against Human Trafficking' (SAPAHT) was constituted to fight trafficking of women and children and enhance cross-border collaboration and information exchange.

There are major international standards which provide a framework within which the countries can address the issue of trafficking. These are :

(1) The United Nations Conventions for the suppression of the traffic in persons and of the exploitation of the prostitution of others 1949. The convention has been ratified by 71 countries (1997), but has not attracted widespread support.

(2) The Convention on the Elimination of all forms of Discrimination against women (CEDAW) 1979. CEDAW obliges states to enact states legislation to suppress all forms of traffic in women. The convention has been ratified by 155 countries (1997).

(3) The United Nations Convention on the rights of the child (CRC) 1989. It has near universal ratification and 189 states are parties to it. Articles 33, 34, 35 and 39 of the convention prohibit trafficking in children.

Though most of the countries of South Asia are signatories to different international conventions and national legislation too has been enacted, implementation remains very weak. Trafficked women and children are extremely vulnerable to the abuses of the legal system. In India about 4 times as many women than men in the sex trade are arrested. Procurers, guardians, pimps and clients are barely touched. Further, the stigma associated with HIV / AIDS has undermined attempts both to repatriate trafficked women as well as to rehabilitate them. Though trafficking is undertaken on a large organised scale involving regional gangs with links to law enforcement agencies, there is no proper regional mechanism to ensure co-operation and co-ordinated action. In the SAARC Summit in Male September 2000, the member-countries agreed to work together to eliminate trafficking. Unfortunately, ratification of the proposed SAARC convention on trafficking and sexual exploitation in women and children adopted at the ministerial meeting in Colombo in July 1998 has been stalled due to the postponement of 1999 SAARC summit.

To combat trafficking in persons, specially "in sex trade, slavery and non-voluntary servitude, the American Congress has now passed an Act known as the 'Trafficking Victims Protection Act 2000'. The Act prescribes minimum standards for elimination of trafficking. The Act lays down that USA will not provide non-humanitarian, non-trade related foreign assistance to any government that does not comply with minimum standards for the elimination of trafficking and is not making significant efforts to bring itself into compliance with such standards.

9

WOMEN PRISONERS*

Prisons constitute a very critical area of human rights concern. A person in custody in any civilised society cannot be reduced to the status of a non-person because he is in prison. Hence, prison system must offer conditions that are compatible with human dignity and conducive to social mainstreaming. Article 10 of the International Covenant on Civil and Political Rights mandates that 'All persons deprived of liberty shall be treated with humanity and with respect for the inherent dignity of the person'. The United Nations Standard Minimum Rules for Protection of Prisoners, known as the (Standard Minimum Rules), adopted by the U.N. Social Economic Council in 1957, provide guidelines for treatment of prisoners and reaffirm the tenet that the prisoners do retain their fundamental rights while in custody. The Supreme Court of India, in the case of Prem Shankar Shukla *versus* Delhi Administration, reaffirmed the principle that "the goal of imprisonment is not only punitive, but restorative, to make an offender a non-offender."

In India the prison population is relatively small, approximately 2,79,082. The situation in India in this respect is to be juxtaposed against those in some of the developed countries. A report of the Bureau of Statistics of the U.S. Department of Justice shows that as on December 1998, there were 1.5 million prisoners in different prisons in the U.S. This gives the U.S.A. a national incarceration rate of 628 prisoners per 1,00,000 against India's 28 prisoners per 1,00,000 population.

Unfortunately, human rights of persons languishing as

---

* Appeared in *The Statesman* on 20-4-2001 & 21-4-2001.

prisoners are often disregarded and violated and women prisoners in this regard suffer the most. Female prisoners constitute a small proportion of the total prison population of the country. Out of the prison population of 2,79,082, the number of women prisoners is approx. 9,233. In prisons in different countries of the world, women remain in small minority. This relatively low proportion of women population in prison has been attributed to various factors like women's innate nature, their domestic status, putative weaknesses, ambiguity regarding their public and legal responsibilities, etc. Unfortunately, this minority status of women in prisons tends to reinforce their lost status. "It is the small number of women in prisons", says the All India Committee for Jail Reforms 1980-83 (better known as 'Mulla Committee') "which in our view is responsible for their needs being neglected. The position of the women scattered in small clusters in jails is highly vulnerable."

In India as early as in 1919-20, the Indian Jails Committee had recommended that structurally separate jails or at least separate enclosures for women prisoners should be so constructed so that "female prisoners or lady visitors entering the jail should be able to reach the female yard without coming under the observation of male prisoners." Unfortunately, condition in this respect has registered very little improvement. In most of the jails of the country whether central prisons, district prisons or sub-jails women prisoners have to walk through men's sections and undergo very humiliating experience oftentimes.

The Indian Jail Committee further argued strongly in favour of creating one or more institutions for convicted women prisoners in each State and concentrate women offenders there from all over the State. The Committee felt that removal of women offenders from their home towns was a lesser evil than allowing them to languish in miserable conditions in some corners of the jails in their own districts. The Commission stressed the need for proper classifications of prisoners and separating women adolescents from old convicted prisoners, prostitutes and procurers from women who have lived hitherto a respectful life. Unfortunately, State governments have paid scant attention to these recommendations.

Many of the women prisoners in Indian jails come from poor and disadvantaged sections of the society. "They are the disadvantaged losers in our complex and competitive society". Women have the added problem of responsibility for their dependents and many do not have the skill of legal employment after serving the term of imprisonment. Women prisoners also suffer from unhealthy living conditions, exploitation and separation from their families. I still recollect how in a Naribandiniketan in Lucknow a number of women prisoners undergoing long terms of imprisonment told me with great anguish that they had not heard anything from their children and family members for a long time. They were particularly very anxious to know about the fate of their daughters. There is need to ensure that women prisoners get frequent opportunities to unite with members of their families.

The Mulla Committee on Jail Reforms expressed the view that to have separate jails for 5 to 6 women offenders in different sub-divisional jails is administratively difficult and financially unviable. Again, the arrangement of concentrating of all women prisoners in one jail can be faulted on the ground that this arrangement keeps women prisoners hailing from distant places separated from their kith and kin. In this connection it may be mentioned that in Russia, women are held in separate prison camps exclusively for them. This means they are held, sometimes, thousands of kilometres away from their homes. In Russia, while there are 5 different levels of security for men prisoners, for women there are only two regimes — general regimes for first offenders and strict regimes for "dangerous recidivists". Often these dangerous women recidivists turn out to be persistent shop-lifters and other petty offenders.

Again, undertrial women prisoners constitute more than 80 per cent of the female jail population of the country. There are undertrial women languishing for more than 4 years in jails for offences for which the sentences may be less if they had been convicted. Moreover, many women prisoners continue in jails for very long periods as they are unable to defend themselves and ignorant of rules and laws of prison. As a result, they are totally at the mercy of the jail officers. The National Expert Committee of Women Prisoners, under the chairmanship of Justice Krishna Ayyar (1987), stated after visiting many women prisoners that both the prisoners and prison staff suffered from "the pathology of mis-information and ignorance of rights and limitations". This often leads to callous disregard of human rights. Similarly, courts also often fail to show proper awareness of the problems of women, specially those with minor children or with bread earning responsibilities in female-headed households. They are, as stated in the report of the Krishna Ayyar Committee, "a low dispositional priority and receive routine neglect".

The National Human Rights Commission members and officers visiting different jails have noted with dismay that there is no pre-release planning and a well-laid policy for rehabilitation of women prisoners after they are released. Indeed, the women offenders in India often face serious problems of rehabilitation during their post-release period. They become vulnerable to suspicion and stigmatisation for being in prison. Again, imprisonment has more adverse effects on women than men. The society considers them as pariahs. Some of the women prisoners in jails said to us that their husbands no longer accepted them and indeed they had no other place to go. They faced a grim and very pathetic situation.

A number of women prisoners suffer from mental depression and other forms of psychiatric illness. In most of the jails in the country, there is no arrangement for psychiatric treatment and counselling. In the report on women prisoners in Indian jails, the National Commission for Women pointed out that in many jails proportion of female prisoners suffering from mental depression was high compared to the male prisoners. There were hardly any arrangements for psychiatric treatment and counselling; ailments of women prisoners were routinely attended. Krishna Ayyar Committee noted that lack of psychiatric attention in prisons was a serious shortfall and affected the well-being of the female prisoners. The Committee suggested that for women prisoners, there should be special arrangement for all necessary pre-natal and post-natal care and treatment.

Women in prisons also suffer various kinds of abuses. Abuse of women prisoners has often been a feature of treatment of women who have lost their liberty. Vivien Stern, in her book *Sin Against the Future*, says that in developing countries the rule that women should guard women is widely followed. Male staff are not admitted to the women section or perform duties with women prisoners. In developed countries the rule is seen as in conflict with equal opportunities legislation but not followed. The deployment of male staff to women prisoners is widespread and brings many problems. In 1996, the Human Rights Watch, an NGO group in the USA, published a report on sexual abuse of women prisoners in state prisons in the U.S.A. It was based on research carried out for more than two years in different prisons in the U.S.A. The report found that "the male prisons staff had vaginally, anally and orally raped woman prisoners and sexually assaulted and abused them. They had used their power over the prisoners to barter excess of goods and privileges for sexual favours." They had taken advantage of their position to spy on them whilst they were undressing in their living rooms or in bath rooms. They had subjected women to verbal degradation and harassment.

In the U.S.A. courts have been receptive to the claims of female prisoners that their conditions of confinement should be equal to that of their male counterparts. Thus, markedly unfair conditions in women prisons in comparison to men's prisons have been held to violate the equal protection clause of the 14th amendment. In the case of Cauterino *vs*. Wilson, the court held that the officials of the Kentucky Department of Correction unconstitutionally discriminated against the inmates of Kentucky's only prison for women. Among the equal protection violations were found inferior programmes, training, vocational education when compared to those available to similarly situated inmates at the state male correctional institutions. Similarly, healthcare needs of family prisoners must comfort with the American Supreme Court decisions in Estella *vs*. Gamble. This decision lays down that the prison officials are in violation of Eighth Amendment Principle against unnecessary infliction of pain when they show a deliberate indifference to the serious medical needs of the prisoners.

Children of women prisoners pose another problem. Children, who are born in jails and those who accompany their mothers in jails, are compelled to live behind the bars without being offenders. They spend the formative years of their lives behind walls of the jails and are the victims of cruel circumstances. A research study on the status of children of women prisoners in Indian jails, done by Prof. B.N. Chattoraj of the National Institute of Criminology and Forensic Science (NICFS), points out that except the provision in the jail manuals that these children should be provided with diet and clothes by jail authorities, there is no Act in the country to take care of this particular category of children. They should be considered as neglected children as stipulated in the Juvenile Justice Act and the benefits of the Act should be made available to them. It is also necessary that in every jail, where children are living with their mothers, should have a creche with qualified staff. This will not only enable the mothers to work during the day, but will also provide proper care to the children by trained staff. Jail authorities should consider collaboration with suitable N.G.Os. to make this facility available to the children of the women prisoners.

For properly appreciating the problems of women prisoners, the fact has to be borne in mind that women prisoners have an entirely different criminal profile from the male prisoners and their social reality is substantially different from that of men. This difference should be reflected in their treatment in the Criminal Justice System, and particularly in their treatment in prisons. Women commit far less violent and serious crimes and far less frequently than men, and they re-offend and abscond less when they are released temporarily from prison. These apply particularly to women who have children they love and want to see. A gender specific policy, based on substantive equality, should acknowledge that women are the primary carers of most of the children in society. It should also note that imprisoned women receive far less support from their partners than the male prisoners receive.

It has been correctly said that the problems of women prisoners have not been properly and clearly dealt with. The history of imprisonment of women is the history of dealing with ambiguity. The prisons, where women have been held, have aped men's prisons and the rules they have been subjected are men's prison rules with slight concessions. They remain, as a Nigerian civil rights organisation described them, "as the prisoners in the shadows".

10

MENTALLY SICK PRISONERS

Prison occupies a critical area of human rights concern. A person in custody is not reduced to the status of a non-person. He is entitled to all human rights, as the Supreme Court has laid down, other than those curtailed by the problems of incarceration itself Unfortunately, inmates of the Indian prisons suffer outrageous violation of their rights. A large number of mentally ill prisoners also languish in jails in contravention of their human rights.

The Chairperson of the National Human Rights Commission, Justice Shri Ranganath Misra, as early as on 11th September 1996 in a letter to all the Chief Ministers clearly indicated that mentally ill persons should not be lodged in jails along with other ordinary prisoners. The Mental Health Act of 1987, which repealed the Lunacy Act 1977, does not permit mentally ill persons to be put in prisons. In his letter, he clearly stated that no mentally ill persons should be permitted to be kept in jails after 1st November 1998. The Commission made clear that it would detail its officers to inspect as many jails as possible and if any mental patient is found detained in such jails, the NHRC would award compensation to the mentally ill persons or members of their families and ask the State government to recover the amount from the delinquent public officials.

Recently, the present Chairperson of the National Human Rights Commission, Justice Shri J. S. Verma, has again reiterated the same instructions and drawn attention of all the Chief Ministers to the fact that lodging of mentally ill persons in prisons is a violation of the provisions of the Mental Health Act of 1987. The NHRC also sought information on the number of mentally sick prisoners languishing in prisons in different States. The details received by the Commission so far from the different States are as follows:

1.	Assam	–	38
2.	Jammu and Kashmir	–	24
3.	Karnataka	–	69
4.	Tamil Nadu	–	3
5.	Delhi	–	38
6.	West Bengal	–	112
7.	Orissa	–	63
8.	Rajasthan	–	92
9.	Manipur	–	26
10.	Sikkim	–	1

States like Andhra Pradesh, Bihar, Goa, Maharashtra, Tripura, Chandigarh, etc. have informed the NHRC that there are no mentally afflicted persons in the jails. Replies from other States have not so far been received. The Commission has again held out the warning that its officers and special representatives would visit some of the jails for monitoring implementation of this recommendation. It is hoped that the State governments will sincerely try to implement the recommendations of the Commission.

It is a fact that many of the mentally affected persons are languishing in prisons without care and attention. The State governments cannot escape from their obligation, as the NHRC has pointed out, to provide psychiatric treatment to the mentally ill. Standard Minimum Rules for the Treatment of Prisoners (adopted at the U.N. Congress on the Prevention of Crime and Treatment of Offenders held in 1955 and approved by Economic and Social Council on 31st July 1957) provide for the psychiatric treatment of insane and mentally abnormal prisoners. Rule 82 of the Standard Minimum Rules provides that prisoners, who suffer from mental diseases or abnormalities, shall be observed and treated in specialised institutions under proper medical management. Again, the medical and psychiatric service of penal institutions shall provide for the psychiatric treatment of all other prisoners, who are in need of such treatment. To comply with the Rules 82 and 83 of the Standard Minimum Rules, a relaxed atmosphere is a basic requirement. It should be characterised by the caring attitudes of the staff and procedures ensuring that prisoners' requests and prison officers reports are taken seriously and acted upon properly. Only in such situation, it may be possible to detect the prisoners who are in need of psychiatric care in the first place. In order to guarantee adequate attention and treatment, it is of special importance to keep correctly and properly the records of the mentally disturbed persons or those who show abnormal conduct.

In any prison the saddest group of prisoners are those suffering from mental illness. Unfortunately, not only in India, but also in prisons in different countries of the world, these mentally unbalanced prisoners, whose problems call for care in hospital instead are locked in cells. Sometimes they are to be found in padded cells and tied up with chains. Again, many prisoners, because of oppressive and suffocating conditions in jails, develop mental illness.

Prison Manuals of different states lay down rules for dealing with the lunatics lodged in prisons. If an undertrial prisoner becomes mentally ill, I.G. of Prisons should move for the removal of the prisoner to the appropriate mental hospital as soon as accommodation is available. Pending the availability of such accommodation, the Inspector General will take steps to order the removal of the prisoner to the prescribed institutions earmarked for the custody of such prisoners. Unfortunately, very often there is inadequacy of accommodation in mental asylums and hospitals and mentally deranged prisoners continue to languish in jails. Moreover, if a prisoner becomes insane after admission in prison or a criminal lunatic is admitted to a prison, a report regarding his case shall be immediately submitted by the Jail Superintendent to the Inspector General for his removal to a mental hospital. There are cases where recovered criminal lunatics come back to jails prior to their ultimate release. In suitable cases government should consider remission of the unexpired portion of their sentences.

Recommendations of the Mulla Committee

All India Committee on Jail Reforms 1980-83 (better known as Mulla Committee) pointed out that all criminal lunatics under the observation of the psychiatrist should be kept in one barrack. If a criminal lunatic underwent trial and was declared "guilty but insane", he should be sent to nearest hospital for further management. And if a criminal lunatic after standing trial following his recovery from his mental illness was declared guilty of the crime, he should undergo the term in prison under the care of the psychiatrist. Such prisoners after recovery should not be kept in prison hospital, but should remain in barracks with other normal inmates.

The Committee further recommended that in addition to regular psychiatrist wings of prison hospitals, there should be in each state one separate prison hospital with capacity of 100 inmates fully equipped for the care and confinement of the criminal lunatics. A psychiatrist should be in charge of the institution. The Mulla Committee during its visits to prisons found that in one prison there were as many as 600 non-criminal lunatics consisting of one-third of the population of the prison. In another State out of a prison population of 10,618, there were as many as 1,301 non-criminal lunatics. In many jails there were no psychiatrists and the mental patients were given tranquillizers and all forms of drug treatment, but electro convulsive therapy was not being administered because it was prohibited in prisons.

It is worthwhile to mention in this connection that schizophrenia and other mental illnesses are a significant problem in prisons in the U.S.A. Infamous 1990 case Madrid *vs*. Gomez showed how isolation techniques used to control California prisoners made those suffering from mental illness more violent. The judge found that the Department of Corrections (DOC) was grossly negligent in its attention to and treatment of the mentally ill prisoners. California had an estimated 10,000 mentally ill prisoners as of 1994 with approximately 1,100 of HIV positive. Gomez and similar law suits have confirmed prisoners reasonable fears of retaliation, brutality and harsh treatment at the hands of the guards who are generally held not accountable.

A large number of mentally ill prisoners are women. The National Committee on Women Prisoners (better known as Krishna Ayyar Committee) recommended the following:

(a) Mentally disturbed women shall not be detained in prison and they shall be given proper treatment in mental hospitals. Those, who are currently in prison, should be immediately transferred to mental health asylums.

(b) At no time mentally ill women shall be left unguarded by women escorts or guards.

(c) Institutional facilities in accordance with Mental Health Act should be established in every State for rendering psychiatric justice to patients.

(d) Conditions in mental hospitals should strictly conform to the medical standards and supervisory staff should be held responsible for ensuring them. Unfortunately, conditions in most of the mental homes are poor. The State governments have not taken worthwhile steps to improve them. In the therapy and rehabilitation of mentally ill women, their families shall be consulted and closely associated wherever possible.

(e) Training should be given to custodial as well as medical staff in mental homes to understand and deal sensitively with the mentally ill persons.

Unfortunately, most of these recommendations for care and treatment of the mentally sick prisoners remain unimplemented. The NHRC's interventions have not so far stirred the State governments to meaningful corrective measures. However, only a vigorous watchdog role by the NHRC and State Human Rights Commissions can spur the State governments to undertake measures to mitigate the agony and sufferings of the mentally sick prisoners. The chances of Central and State governments taking meaningful initiatives on their own are slim.

11

COMPLAINTS AGAINST THE POLICE : Investigatory Role of the National Human Rights Commission

The National Human Rights Commission (NHRC) was set up under the Protection of Human Rights Act, 1993 for the protection and promotion of human rights in India. One of the important functions of the Commission, as outlined in Section-12A of the Act, is to enquire into the violation of human rights and abetment thereof, and (negligence in the prevention of such violation by a public servant. Since its inception the NHRC had started receiving numerous complaints of violation of human rights from all over the country. A large number of such complaints concern violation of human rights by the police. The number of complaints registered in the NHRC during the year 1996-97 was 16,823 and 31,299 in 1997-98. In 1999 it jumped up to 54,236. Complaints of various sorts ranging from simple to odious against the police and the security personnel now constitute more than half of the total number of complaints being received at the Commission. Some of the complaints against the police are frivolous, vexatious and often engineered by the criminal elements for discomfiting the police. Nevertheless, there are also many true cases of serious violation of human rights by the police which include arbitrary arrest, implication in false cases, misconduct and misbehaviour towards women and custodial violence.

One of the important instructions issued by the NHRC immediately after its constitution was that deaths in police custody should be reported to it within 24 hours. The Commission's letter mentions that failure to report such cases within 24 hours will lead to a presumption that the authorities are trying to suppress the facts. During the period from 1.4.95 to 31.3.96, 136 deaths in police custody were reported to the Commission and the figure shot up to 188 during the period from 1.4.96 to 31.3.97 and in the period from 1.4.97 to 31.3.98, 193 cases of deaths in police custody were reported. All cases of death in police custody do not invariably mean torture or violence by the police, but in quite a few cases deaths in police lock-ups due to torture and misuse of force by the police have come to light.

In a number of serious offences of misuse of authority and commission of custodial crimes by the police, the NHRC first asked for reports from the State authorities and finding that the reports were inadequate or revealed attempts to cover up the lapses of the police officers, it had to order investigation of the cases by its own staff. The Protection of Human Rights Act (HRC), Section 11(1)(B) provides that the Commission will have its own investigative staff under an officer not below the rank of the Director General of Police and such other officers and staff as may be necessary for the efficient performance of the functions of the Commission. I was the first Director General and remained incharge of the Investigation Wing of the National Human Rights Commission for more than four years.

In this connection it may be mentioned that police officers in different countries of the world have never appreciated or approved investigation into cases of complaints against the police by an outside agency. They view it as some sort of interference in the internal management of the police. Even upright senior officers also feel that police misconduct can be controlled only through vigorous internal regulation. They are of the view that senior officers have a nose for bad apples while having a sympathetic understanding of stresses and strains that cause police misconduct. Outsiders will fail on both counts and end up being both ineffective and unfair. There is also the danger that the police officers are like to close ranks and try to screen the offenders from scrutiny by an outside agency. However, experience in different democratic countries of the world has shown that exclusive reliance on police regulation is not sufficient to check misuse of police powers and that is the reason why civilian oversight of the police has emerged as one of the legitimate means by which the State authorities try to ensure check on abuse or misuse of police powers.

It is normally very difficult to substantiate complaints against the police personnel. Very often the malpractice occurs in the police territory and the officers who break the laws have all the opportunities to hide their misdeeds. There is also the code of silence among the police officers. This is the reason why unsubstantiated complaints against the police should be considered as complaints that lack adequate evidence to support rather than unjustified complaints. Initially, senior police officers and their political masters viewed the NHRC as a police-bashing agency. In many meetings senior police officers expressed their grievance that only the police had been singled out as the violator of human rights. It had to be painstakingly explained to them that the violation of human rights are committed by many other agencies of the government, but violation by the police are far more serious and sinister because they deprive the people of their rights to life and liberty and leave behind scars which take long time to heal. Our efforts in the NHRC from the beginning was to carry the police leadership with us while enquiring into the complaints against the police and also to make clear that the object was not just to punish the officers but ensure compliance with rules and laws by the police. Willing compliance is always to be preferred to the exacted deterrence.

Case of Atal Bihari Mishra

Whenever instances of serious misconduct by the police came to light during investigation by the NHRC officers, the Commission in many cases asked the State CID to undertake further investigation and report to the Commission. One such well-known and important case was the custodial death in Ballia (Uttar Pradesh) of one Atal Bihari Mishra, a student of Banaras Hindu University. The former Prime Minister, Chandrasekhar, raised the matter in the Parliament and urged the government to refer the case to the NHRC. Initially, the district police tried to show that the death of Mishra was caused by a bomb attack by some hoodlums on the vehicle he was travelling. Investigation by the Senior Superintendent of Police of the Commission revealed that Mishra was implicated in a false case and tortured to death in the police station because of the political differences between his father and a local politician belonging to the then ruling party in U.P.

At the instance of the Commission, the State CID took up the investigation and submitted a chargesheet against as many as 19 police officers, including the Superintendent of Police. The Commission further directed the State government to pay to the father of the deceased a sum of Rs. 5 lakhs by way of interim compensation. It also urged the Government of U.P. to consider sympathetically the prayer of the family for an appointment at an appropriate level having regard to the eligibility and qualifications of a suitable member of the family on compassionate grounds. The Government of Uttar Pradesh took the stand that as the case of Atal Bihari Mishra was pending in the court of Chief Judicial Magistrate, Ballia, compliance of the recommendations of the Commission could be possible only after the police officials accused were found guilty of the charges. The Commission considered the stand taken by the State government as incorrect and pointed out that the award of interim relief under Sub-Section 3 of Section 18 of the Protection of the Human Rights Act, 1993 is not dependent upon the establishment of the culpability of the public servant. The remedy is "independent of such pettifoggeries". The Commission pointed out that "the meaning to be given to Section 18(3) by any state professing to be a welfare state should ensure a liberal construction to promote the philosophy of the statute and to advance its beneficent and benevolent purposes. The view that implies that administration of such "immediate interim relief' could only be at the end of the day, after the guilt of the offending public servant is established in a criminal trial on the standards of criminal evidence would nullify the great humanism the statute seeks to enshrine. The Commission only hopes that the Government of Uttar Pradesh is an ally of those values and will respond in a way which accords with the message and philosophy of the law and its obligation as a welfare state". The Government of Uttar Pradesh subsequently paid the compensation to the victim's family as recommended by the Commission.

There was another unfortunate case of the death of one Usman Ansari of Nagpur, where the Commission had to intervene because senior police officials were trying to cover up the misdeeds of their subordinates. In this case the Commission received a complaint from Smt. Hamida Begam, a resident of Nagpur, alleging that her husband Usman Ansari was forcibly taken by four police constables from their home to prepare food for a party that was organised to celebrate the promotion of the Head Constable as Sub-Inspector. Next morning, the dead body of her husband was found on the road near the place where the party was held.

In response to the Commission's notice the Director General of Police, Maharashtra informed the Commission that the investigation of the case was closed by State CID as nobody could give definite clues which would help to detect the culprits. The Commission found the report of the State CID as unsatisfactory and directed its own investigating officers to enquire into the matter. The Investigation Division's report pointed out that investigation by the State CID was perfunctory and an attempt had been made to cover up the facts. The Commission's investigation further revealed that a scuffle had taken place between the deceased and some policemen who had come to attend the party and the deceased had sustained an injury on the skull which caused his death. Death was not caused because of the road accident. The Commission asked the Government of Maharashtra to get the matter investigated by the CBI and to pay a compensation of Rs. 2 lakhs to the next of kin of the victim. The Commission directed that the amount so paid may subsequently be recovered from those police personnel whose guilt will be established from an independent investigation.

Decisive investigation of the NHRC in a case of the killing of a businessman at Ranchi had a salutary impact. The Commission received a complaint from one Reeta Dhawan of Ranchi that the Maruti van of her husband, while he was returning from Varanasi, was surrounded by six policemen near the Police Civil Lines, Ranchi. They demanded Rs. 1 lakh and on being refused shot at the petitioner's husband and others from a point blank range and killed them. This happened on December 5, 1993. They also removed the gold chain, rings and wrist watch from the body of the deceased. At Commission's instance a criminal case was started against the police officers who were suspended. In the case the officers were convicted and sentenced to death. The Commission also directed that an immediate payment of Rs. 10 lakhs should be awarded to Reeta Dhawan without prejudice to her private law rights for damages. The State government contended that as the accused persons have already been convicted and sentenced to death, the government found no justification for paying a compensation of Rs. 10 lakhs as this will cause an unnecessary financial burden on the State. The Commission pointed out that stand of the government was incorrect. The establishment of a culpability of public servants in a criminal trial and their conviction does not put at rest the claim for compensation or immediate relief to the dependents of the victims as envisaged in the Section 18(3) of the Protection of Human Rights Act. The establishment of culpability of the involved public servants cannot absolve the State of its liability for compensation. The State government complied with the recommendations of making payment to Reeta Dhawan.

In another case concerning high-handedness of PAC personnel at Varanasi, the Commission took *suo-motu* cognisance of a newspaper report which appeared in *The Pioneer* dated 05.08-97 under the caption "Students face PAC jawans' wrath". In this case also investigation done by the officers of the Investigation Division of the Commission established the high-handedness on the part of PAC personnel in confining and assaulting a group of students who had gathered to felicitate a friend on his academic achievement. Later on, at the instance of the Commission, the State CID took up the investigation of the case and submitted a charge-sheet against 28 PAC personnel for various offences under the Indian Penal Code in the court of the Chief Judicial Magistrate, Varanasi. Again, taking into account the unprovoked nature of the attack and wrongful confinement, the likely cost of medical treatment involved and the violation of the dignity and integrity of the person, the Commission recommended interim compensation by way of immediate relief as per Sub-Section 3 of Section 18 under the Protection of Human Rights Act, 1993. The compensation amount for each of the students ranged between Rs.10,000 to Rs.25,000. The Government of U.P. has confirmed that the sanction has been accorded by the Governor of U.P. for the payment of immediate relief to the victims as directed by the Commission.

Video-Filming of Post-Mortem Examinations

The NHRC also felt concerned at the uneven quality of post-mortem reports. A number of instances came to the Commission's notice where post-mortem reports appeared to have been doctored due to the influence of the officials who perpetrated the offence. There was also inordinate delay in writing of the post-mortem reports. In cases of custodial deaths, very often the fate of cases depends upon the opinions given by the doctors in the post-mortem reports. There can be total miscarriage of justice if the reports are manipulated and the doctors intimidated. The Commission, therefore, recommended "video-filming" of post-mortem examinations and sending of tapes to the Commission for scrutiny with a view to preventing such malpractices. Twenty-two States and Union territories have now accepted the recommendations while two others have stated that they are examining the matter. The Commission is pressing upon the remaining States to accept its recommendations without any further delay. The Commission also circulated for adoption a model autopsy form that took into consideration the work done by the United Nations on the subject and special circumstances prevailing in the country. Seventeen States and Union territories have accepted the model autopsy form and the concomitant procedures recommended by the Commission.

Visits to the Police Lock-ups

Disturbed by increasing reports of violence in the police lock-ups, the Commission decided that its officers will make visits to the police lock-ups. Section 12C of the Protection of Human Rights Act provides that the Commission shall visit under intimation to the State government any jail or institution under the control of the State government where persons are detained or lodged for purposes of proper treatment, reformation or protection and also to study the living conditions of the inmates and make recommendations thereon. The Secretary-General of the Commission wrote to the Chief Secretaries of the States to issue necessary instruction to enable the officers of the NHRC to visit the State to undertake visits to police lock-ups as well. Twenty-six States/Union territories have since accepted the suggestion. The Commission is pursuing this matter with the governments of Arunachal Pradesh, Assam, Jammu & Kashmir, Manipur and the Union territories of Daman and Diu who are yet to respond positively. The Commission also issued detailed instruction to the officers of its Investigation Division regarding the manner in which they are to inspect the lock-ups. A list of "dos and don'ts" have been prepared and circulated to the NHRC officers.

Human Rights Cells

The Commission has also now urged the Police administration in the States to set up Human Rights Cells in the Police Headquarters, which will serve as the main link between the NHRC and the State police agencies. This Police Complaints Authority at State Police Headquarters will function as an oversight body. It will also take steps to ensure human rights training and sensitisation of the police officers and men, organise seminars and workshops on human rights in association with the State Human Rights Commissions and the NHRC, and actively promote human rights, literacy and awareness through different seminars and workshops.

The Commission has further strongly felt the need for systemic reforms in the police. It has emphasised the need for implementing speedily some of the important recommendations of the National Police Commission for insulating the police from external pressures and influence and for building up of some institutional mechanisms to depoliticise the police. The Commission felt gratified when the then Home Minister, Indrajit Gupta, in a letter to Chief Ministers of States in 1997 chose to pursue the matter and fully endorse the recommendations of the National Human Rights Commission and the National Police Commission for systemic reforms in police. The Commission also impleaded itself as a party in the case of Prakash Singh *Vs.* Union of India and others before the Supreme Court of India which relates specifically to the implementation of the recommendations of the National Police Commission. In a comprehensive affidavit the Commission highlighted the need for insulation of the police from extraneous pressures and other structural reforms so that the police is not utilised by the party in power to subserve its own ends. The Commission looks forward to the verdict of the Supreme Court which will have an important bearing on systemic police reforms and help the police to uphold law and protect human rights with greater competence.

12

NATIONAL HUMAN RIGHTS COMMISSION'S INTERVENTIONS FOR PRISON REFORMS

Prisons constitute a critical area of human rights concern. A prisoner, just because he is in prison, is not reduced to the status of a non-person. The goal of imprisonment, to quote the words of Justice Krishna Iyer in the case of Prem Shankar Shukla *Vs* Delhi Administration, is "not only punitive but restorative, to make an offender a non-offender". The United Nations Standard Minimum Rules for Protection of Prisoners adopted by the U.N. Social and Economic Council in 1957 provided guidelines for treatment of prisoners and reaffirmed the tenet that prisoners did retain their fundamental rights even while in custody.

At present, in India, the total number of prisons, including central prisons, district prisons, sub-jails, etc., is 1306 and the total prison population (as on 31.12.98) was 2,57,235. Seventy-three per cent of the prisoners are undertrials and majority of these undertrials come from disadvantaged sections of the society with rural background.

In India the Prison Administration is governed by the Prison Act of 1894. The Act is old and many of its provisions are outdated and ante-diluvian. Section 27 of this old Act provides that unconvicted prisoners ought to be kept apart from the convicted prisoners. Many jail manuals also provide for segregation of the undertrials from the convicted prisoners. However, there are no separate buildings for keeping the undertrial prisoners and so willy-nilly, they are confined for long periods in the same prison building along with the convicted inmates.

Lodging undertrial prisoners along with convicted criminals results in "contamination of crime". Many inexperienced young men come in touch with the hardened criminals and get coarsened, brutalised and criminalised. It is known that many gangsters recruit the members of their criminal gangs from out of these "borderline and yet redeemable" offenders admitted to jails. Many of these undertrials are also carriers of contraband goods as well as contagious diseases. The National Human Rights Commission (NHRC) had strongly recommended that there should be separate institutions for accommodating undertrial prisoners with adequate security and segregation facilities at each place where a central or district prison is located. This will relieve pressure on central and district prisons. These institutions should also be located near the court premises to reduce the problems and hazards of transporting the prisoners.

A frequent complaint, which the NHRC gets from the prisoners, regarding the quality and quantity of food served to them. In the restricted environment of prison, where the prisoners do not get the food of their own choice and liking, the quality of food served to them becomes an important issue. The NHRC officers in the course of their visits to different prisons have found that prison kitchens are dirty and the manner of preparation of food for the prisoners is unhygienic and dirty. Many prisoners suffering from disease and not knowing cooking at all are compelled to cook food. In many prisons food of inferior quality is given to the prisoners who fall foul of the prison staff. The NHRC has recommended that the ways and means of privatising the catering service in the prisons should be examined and the work of preparing food for the prisoners should be entrusted to responsible NGO groups. Similarly, the West Bengal Human Rights Commission in its Annual Report 1997-98 while noting the decline in the quality of "supplies and services" in jails, suggested that a time has come when the government may "seriously consider to entrust some of the jail services to reputed NGOs, philanthropic bodies and organisations of ex-servicemen etc. selectively". Response from the State governments so far has not been encouraging.

Deaths in Prisons

The National Human Rights Commission (NHRC) made an analysis of deaths of prisoners in jails and came to the conclusion that lives of many of the prisoners could have been saved if proper medical examination had been carried out at the time of admission and followed up by periodical medical checks. As per the direction issued by the Commission, cases of death in the police lock-ups and in jails are to be reported to it within 24 hours. During the year 1996-96, 308 cases; in 1996-97, 700 cases and in 1998-99, 1114 cases of death in jail custody were reported to the Commission. A major cause of death in jails is tuberculosis. Because of over-crowding and unhygienic conditions in the prison many prisoners contract this illness and perish. This is also a problem in prisons of many other countries. Tuberculosis is the main killer in many Russian prisons, as mentioned in a report of the Human Rights Watch — a well-known international NGO group. The National Human Rights Commission, with the help of experts, has devised a proforma for health screening of the prisoners and directed the Chief Secretaries of all States on 11.02.99 to ensure that medical examination of all prisoners was carried out in accordance with the proforma. An elaborate proforma for the medical examination was prepared with the help of the experts. The format includes an indication by the examining medical officer as to the medical and diet regimen that should receive particular attention. The format also indicates the need for confirmatory tests. The Commission also directed that monthly reports should be sent to the Commission regarding the medical examination of the prisoners after their initial admission in jails. Though the prison rules require the examination of the prison inmates on or immediately after their admission, conduct of such medical examination is more an exception than the norm.

Non-official Visitors

In another important development, the Bombay High Court in the case of Mukta Ram Sindhe *Vs* State of Maharashtra requested the Commission to appoint non-official visitors for the jails of Maharashtra. Under the Maharashtra Visitors of Prisons Rules, there is a Board of Visitors consisting of ex-officio and non-official visitors in respect of each of the prisons of the State. The court requested the Commission to nominate eminent persons from the field of correctional administration, juvenile welfare for undertaking visits to the jails. Responding to the directions of the court, the Commission nominated persons for 33 prisons of Maharashtra and the State government subsequently notified them as visitors. The non-official visitors acting on behalf of the Commission, is now playing an important role in keeping a watch over prison conditions in Maharashtra. The Commission also formulated detailed guidelines for the nominees who will visit the prisons to find out if the living conditions of the inmates are satisfactory and consistent with human rights. The visitors have also been instructed to bring to the notice of the Commission the aberrations that they noticed and the corrective steps they want the Commission to take.

The National Human Rights Commission brought out a draft guidelines for improving prison conditions. In drafting the guidelines, the Commission consulted a number of NGOs involved in practical prison work and also persons with long practical experience in prison administration. These guidelines have been circulated to all the Inspectors General of Prisons with a view to bringing about improvement in prison conditions.

Checklists

For practical guidance to the officers inspecting jails, the Commission prepared a checklist in consultation with experts regarding the issues to be kept in mind during inspection. Before finalising the checklist the Commission sought and got the comments of IGs of Prisons and other experts. During visits to the prisons in various States, the Commission members as well as the officers observed that Sessions Judges were not visiting the jails in the regular manner as required by the Prison Manual. The Chairperson of the NHRC demi-officially addressed the Chief Justices of High Courts and requested them to give appropriate instruction to the District Sessions Judges to make regular visits to jails in order to review the conditions of the prisoners and also to hold regularly the meeting of the District Committee comprising the District Magistrate, Sessions Judge and the District Superintendent of Police. A number of Chief Justices have informed the Chairman of the Commission that they had issued appropriate instructions.

The Commission also felt that the knowledge of the prison staff regarding prison rules, procedures and the directions of the court is inadequate. Their communication skill and interpersonal management is also very poor. The Commission took initiative in organising training courses for the prison staff in collaboration with the National Institute of Criminology and Forensic Science (NICFS). The efforts of the Commission evoked positive response and now a regular courses for the prison officials are organised by the NICFS.

Undertrials

For improving prison conditions, it is imperative to make very determined efforts to reduce the number of the undertrials in jails. It was hoped that Supreme Court's pathbreaking decision in the case of Common Cause *Vs* Union of India in which the Apex Court prescribed different kinds of cases pending trial where the accused persons can be released on bail. Unfortunately, the judgement of the court is not self-executing and so even after the judgement a large number of prisoners continue to languish in jails because there is nobody to present their cases before the courts. Further, a number of prisoners though granted bail remain imprisoned because there is no one to provide sureties for them.

It also came to the notice of the Commission that though the power of premature release of prisoners undergoing sentence of life-imprisonment is to be exercised by the State government under the provisions of Section 432 of the Criminal Procedure Code, the procedure and practice followed by different State governments are not uniform. The system differs from State to State so far as the eligibility criteria of the persons eligible for consideration of premature release, composition of the Sentence

Review Boards and the guidelines governing the question of premature release. In many States the Sentence Review Boards have not been meeting regularly. The Commission formed a committee comprising its senior officers to evolve a set of recommendations to bring uniformity to the procedure in all the States to be followed. The Commission has now issued detailed guidelines regarding the composition of the State Sentence Review Boards, periodicity of its meetings, eligibility of premature release of prisoners undergoing life-imprisonment and the categories of convicted prisoners who should not be considered for premature release like prisoners convicted of the offence such as rape, dacoity, terrorist crime, professional murderers, etc., and the guidelines to be followed by the Sentence Review Boards.

The NHRC gets petitions from life-convicts over 70 years of age who are languishing in prisons for more than 30 years. A life-convict in the Central Jail in Lucknow told the writer that he remained incarcerated for nearly 30 years. Section 433-A of the Criminal Procedure Code prescribes that "if a person is convicted of an offence for which death is one of the punishments provided by law or where the sentence of death imposed on a person has been commuted under Section 433 of the Criminal Procedure Code into one of imprisonment for life, such person shall not be released unless he had served at least 14 years of imprisonment". This Section of the Criminal Procedure Code in the opinion of Justice A.M. Mullah Committee on Jail Reforms had the effect of sacrificing "the values of rehabilitation and reformation on the lifers altogether". In selected cases the power of the Governor to grant pardon can be effected under Section 161 of the Constitution so that the prisoners can be released even before completing 14 years of imprisonment. However, it has been noticed that even exercise of this power by the Governor for premature release of the prisoners has not been based upon objective criteria.

The difficulties of the prisoners in getting parole have come to the Commission's notice in a number of cases. In one particular case (No. 8572/95-96/NHRC), Harbhajan Singh, a convict undergoing life imprisonment in Central Jail in Bikaner levelled corruption charges against the Superintendent of the Central Jail, Bikaner. He alleged that when he requested for the grant of parole to make arrangements for the medical treatment of his wife, the Superintendent of Jail had given a wrong report that the complainant was planning to leave the country. The Jail Administration in its report to the Commission admitted that there had been a mix-up of papers of the two prisoners with the identical name and the Superintendent of Jail sought to explain it as a clerical error and said that when the mistake was noticed, grant of parole was recommended to the District Magistrate. The Commission was not satisfied with the report. Its investigating team investigated into the case and found that the mixing-up of the papers of the two prisoners was not a mere mistake. The investigation revealed that the Jail Superintendent had asked the complainant's son to arrange for Rs. 20,000 and made clear that otherwise his father would face a tough time in jail. A deal was struck for Rs. 14,000 and Rs. 10,000 was paid by the complainant's son through a warder. After a few months the complainant's mother expired. The complainant's father managed to get the parole by making a payment of Rs. 3,000. As the son could not pay the balance amount, the father was tortured. The Commission directed the State government to take appropriate action against the jail officials and pay Rs. 20,000 to the complainant because of deprivation, humiliation and the harassment suffered by him.

Women Prisoners

The Commission had given special attention to the condition of women prisoners. Many of the women prisoners expressed their sad and sorrowful plight to the officers of the Commission. In the Naribandi Niketan of U.P., a number of women prisoners told the present writer that their husbands did not accept them after their release from prisons. They also complained that they rarely heard from their families. There is urgent need to ensure that women prisoners should have frequent opportunities to unite with members of their families. The Commission felt that some of the key recommendations of the National Expert Committee on

Women Prisoners, which met under the chairmanship of Justice V.R. Krishna Iyer in 1986-87, should be followed up with greater vigour. These include the following:

(a) All custodial premises of women prisoners should have secure environment.

(b) There should be schemes for gainful vocational training for the women prisoners. Unfortunately, in many of the jails there are no arrangements for even elementary education of the women prisoners. The NHRC members as well as its officers visiting jails have noted with dismay that there was no pre-release planning and well-laid policy for the rehabilitation of women prisoners after their release. This is necessary because women are stigmatised for being in prison, the society considers them as pariahs. A number of women prisoners suffer from mental depression and other forms of psychosomatic illness. There is hardly any arrangement of psychiatric treatment and counselling for them. Qualified lady doctors and nurses should be attached on a visiting basis to every prison for women and custodial centres for women inmates. Prison administration also has to be more sensitive and responsive to the problems of children of the women prisoners.

INDEX